To Morgan God put us together c u in Boston! or Nashville' [signature] ♥ ii

I Shall Remember Thy Holy Name From
GENERATION TO GENERATION

A Serbian-American Woman Awakens To Christ's Call...

By
Ariane Trifunovic Montemuro
With Tim Weeks

Printed with the blessing of
His Grace
Bishop LONGIN
+ + +

Ideas into Books®
WESTVIEW
P.O. Box 605, Kingston Springs, TN 37082
www.publishedbywestview.com

ISBN 978-1-62880-131-6

First Edition, November 17, 2016

FRONT COVER PHOTOS:
(top right) Ariane's mother Danica as a child with her parents, 1935
(bottom left) Ariane's father Aleksandar as a child with his parents, 1925

COVER & BOOK DESIGN:
Elaine P. Millen, TeknoLink Marketing Services

Photographs on pages 25, 60 (top), 76, 104, and 137 are in the public domain.
All other photographs are from the author's private collection.

The author gratefully acknowledges permission to reprint the lyrics to *Undeniable* on page 133:

Composition: (4182804) *Undeniable* (50%)
Chuck Butler/ Gabriel Patillo/ Jason Ingram/ Toby McKeehan
Controlled Label Copy: Open Hands Music (SESAC)/ So Essential Tunes (SESAC)/
Be Essential Songs (BMI)/ Jord A Lil Music (BMI)
(admin. at www.EssentialMusicPublishing.com). All rights reserved. Used by permission.

Song ID: (109647) *Undeniable* (50%)
Chuck Butler, Gabriel Patillo, Jason Ingram, Toby McKeehan
Copyright © 2015 Achtober Songs (BMI) Universal Music - Brentwood Benson Songs (BMI)
Songs of Gotee (BMI) Patillo Music (BMI) (adm. at CapitolCMGPublishing.com) /
All Essential Music (ASCAP) / So Essential Tunes (SESAC) / Buddybabe Music (ASCAP) /
C/O JASON INGRAM (SESAC) All rights reserved. Used by permission.

Printed in the United States of America on acid-free paper.

**I Shall Remember Thy Holy Name From
Generation To Generation**
www.generationtogenerationbook.com
Brentwood, Tennessee

DEDICATION

I dedicate my book to my great-grandfather, the Very Reverend Trandafil Kocić, a priest who served the Orthodox Church in Leskovac, Serbia.

His beautiful voice was silenced when he and many fellow priests were martyred for the Kingdom of Heaven in Surdulica, Serbia, on November 17, 1915.

Ariane Trifunovic Montemuro

On November 17, 1990,
exactly seventy-five years after his untimely and tragic death,
Ariane and Tony Montemuro were married at
St. Nicholas Serbian Orthodox Church
in Philadelphia, Pennsylvania.

I SHALL REMEMBER THY HOLY NAME FROM
GENERATION TO GENERATION

A SERBIAN-AMERICAN WOMAN AWAKENS TO CHRIST'S CALL...

TABLE OF CONTENTS

BORN FOR ETERNITY

> ❝*The Lord is present everywhere and nothing happens without His will
> or His permission, either in this life or eternity.*❞
> *Serbian Orthodox Elder Thaddeus Vitovnica*[1]

I have always thought that by the time I hit my fifth decade, my life would be pretty well-defined and ordered according to my personal goals and dreams. At this very moment, I have "arrived" at that point and I see that many of my hopes have been achieved. However, something new and unexpected has now popped up for me to ponder in these last few years. I began to earnestly question and sense a strong, almost unstoppable, pull to search for the deeper meaning to my life. Everything was changing…the way I thought, the way I felt. Even the style of my oil paintings was different.

I had not prepared for dealing with my sensitive, stubborn, proud, strong-willed, colorful, fashion diva, five-language-speaking, Sorbonne-educated, Serbian-born mom slipping away rapidly from vascular dementia. My Serbian-born dad died over thirty years ago. Now I feel a new type of solitude. I realize that I am becoming the matriarch of the family. I am the living generational thread to our family history and my Serbian parents and ancestors. I am rapidly becoming the "keeper of stories" as my mother once was. I am the one now to discern which stories are important to keep for my children and which are okay to let go.

By most people's standards, I, Ariane Trifunovic Montemuro, am blessed to be living the "American dream." The daughter of Serbian immigrants to the U.S., I have everything I wished for as a little girl. I have a virtuous, kind, loving, wonderful husband, who is the father to our two beautiful children. We have a well-adjusted, happy family together. Even our dog is my dream dog! But, after achieving all my worldly joy, I've felt a need to find new answers to the timeless question — who am I, really? What is the most precious treasure I am obligated to dutifully pass onto future generations regarding my life? What is my life all about? What is most important to Ariane Trifunovic Montemuro?

This book is about my discovery of the deeper meaning of life. It is essentially about the supreme purpose of my life — or any human life, for that matter. I am not any different from you. My life is just as beautiful and special and joyful as yours. My life has had its share of pain, anger and confusion like yours. I have veered off course just like you. I have felt alone like you. What we have in common is our need to know who created us and what this life is all about. Our entire life is a journey of discovery.

We discover many things along the way. This book is written for only one reason. It is written to remind people of the order of life.

The order of life is God — first and foremost. He is first and nothing happens in your life without the will of God in action. Everything in your life has enormous spiritual meaning according to the will of God. This goes for everything from the timing of things to the significance of dates and people in your life. It even includes the seemingly insignificant parts of our lives. This is what is most important to pass onto future generations. God's living and active presence fills all details of our lives. He is the head of our lives. If we are not pursuing God and seeking Him, what or who are we seeking? Everything else in life falls under that order. Do we live life according to God's commandments? Do we really know who God is: God the Father, the Son, and the Holy Spirit? Our God is Triune. One God in three persons. Do we try to draw near to God by praying or talking to Him and involving Him in every day of our lives? Have we ever opened His book, the Bible, to learn how to live? Do we use it to judge ourselves or simply to judge others? What are we meant to strive for in this lifetime? Simply put, we must constantly work to be aware of the Kingdom to come. This life is only temporary. We are born for eternity.

We all have the same high and important calling no matter who we are. All of us. From generation to generation, we must work out our salvation during this lifetime. We must constantly struggle to draw near to God. This has been the plight of early Christians and it needs to continue to be the goal of the current generation. We must work to preserve the image of Christ in all we do. We must examine our lives as we journey through them. When we look back on our lives one day, will we truly be able to say we tried as much as we could to live our lives as Christ teaches? Are we consciously aware of God's presence in all we do? Do we know what this means?

We must confess and forgive each other and let go of grudges. We must love. Are we working to rid ourselves of our own anger or are we blaming others? Christ gave us the blueprint on how to live. We must align ourselves with the Church to guide us and help us stay on course. We cannot separate the Bible from the Church. If we do, we open the door to confusion and untruth. As a Christian we must know and accept Christ and his teachings and the whole entirety of our Christian faith. But do we even know our ancient Christian faith? St. Paul teaches us: "Therefore, brethren, stand fast, and hold the traditions which ye have been taught, whether by word, or our epistle" (2 Thessalonians 2:15 KJV). Therefore, we cannot separate the Bible from the ancient Holy Tradition of the Church. The Holy Traditions of the Church are both doctrinal and liturgical practices that have been handed down to us since before the completion of the Bible. These traditions express the totality of our Christian way of life that lead to salvation. It is not for us to take away from these traditions nor change them. This is what the Ancient Orthodox Church is.

For 2,000 years, the Church has taught that salvation does not come in one single day or moment. Our entire life is a journey of salvation. We all have the chance to draw near to God each day. Every day we must work to live a Christ-centered life. This is not an easy thing to do. As a first-generation Serbian-American woman, I want my love of God to be a strong link to the next generation. I want to struggle to know God and to live in Christ. It is hard to be in the world, but not of the world. We must preserve our ancient Orthodox Christian faith for the future generations. For many untold centuries my Serbian ancestors fought to preserve their Christian faith and even died for it because they knew this same faith could preserve them. I am grateful to them and I believe their efforts were not in vain.

This book is my offering to God. It is also my statement of appreciation to all the Serbs who gave their lives in defense our Holy Orthodox Christian Faith. I pray that future generations and anyone who reads this book will always remember God first. If I am even remembered for anything, let it be for only inspiring people to struggle to put God first and to always preserve and cherish their unending love for Him in word, deed, and truth forever.

> *God is all there is and all there ever was…*
> *In God I found out who I am and who I need to be…*
> *the living image of Christ.*
> *"…my tongue is the pen of a ready writer."*
> *(Psalm 45:1 KJV)*
> *Glory be to God in all things. Slava Gospodu za sve.*

Ariane Trifunovic Montemuro

Ariane and her family: husband Tony, son Tony, daughter Ana and their Westie dog, MacDuff.

Maka (Grandma) always said, "Krv nije voda (blood is not water)."

This story is a love letter to my children…Tony and Ana Montemuro, grandchildren of Aleksandar and Danica Trifunovic and great-grandchildren of Velibor and Darinka Dobrić and Ljubomir and Vera Trifunović and the great-great grandchildren of the Very Reverend Trandafil and Natalia Kocić and Mihailo and Danica Dobrić. I wrote my story for you. Even as much as Daddy and I love and adore you both, always remember first how very much God loves you! Put God first in all things. While you were in school, I attended church monthly as often as I could to pray with the other parents for all of you, our children. We came together to pray an Akathist, or standing prayer, to the Mother of God, "Nurturer of Children." There is one portion of the prayer that stands out so deeply in my heart I would like to joyfully share it with you. I hope that one day you all will pray this for my grandchildren and great grandchildren and all our future generations…

Ikos 4

Having heard Thy voice, crying to Thy Son, "Preserve in Thine inheritance those whom Thou hast given me unto the ages," I stretch out my hands and my heart towards Thy loving-kindness, entreating that Thou wilt keep my children among Thy servants, and fulfill these my petitions:

Raise my children in Thy most holy inheritance.
Raise my children with all Thy Saints.
Raise my children to be Thy servants, fulfilling all thy commands.
Raise my children to seek help from Thee alone.
Raise my children to inherit eternal life.
Raise my children, O Lady, to be made worthy of the Kingdom of heaven
  and make them heirs of eternal blessings.[1]

Glory be to God always and I love you and my entire family forever.

Mama

KISSES
POLJUPCI

… Kisses of gratitude to my parents who passed their faith to me. …

Mommy and Daddy, 1981, in front of Serbian coat of arms.

SPECIAL

THANKS

I offer my book as a thanks to God first and foremost. Then, I offer it to everyone as a testimony and witness to His glory working in all our lives! I thank God for His never-ending mercy upon me and my life! I pray this extends to my beloved children Tony and Ana and all my future generations!

Secondly, I thank my devoted, loving, loyal husband who exhibits so many beautiful Christian virtues that I have yet to express myself. Throughout our 25 years of marriage, our deep love for each other has always been and will forever be a given. This book would never have come to fruition without my dedicated husband, Anthony Montemuro, M.D., and his unwavering support.

My beautiful mother Danica and my warm-hearted father Aleksandar gave me all they had in terms of love and support to have a better life in their new free country — the United States of America. I would not be who I am without them. I adore them forever.

My beloved in-laws, Pennsylvania State Supreme Court Justice Frank J. Montemuro and Peggy Gigliotti Montemuro, who always treated me with such respect and love.

My older brother Robert who has always looked out for me and helped me. I love you and your family forever. I also thank my brothers-in-law, Frank and Mike, and their families for their love.

My Uncle Mike Dobrich, my Aunt Lela, and my dear cousin Doris Manojlovic and her family for sharing our family history with me.

I thank God for handpicking my co-author Tim Weeks. I could not have found such an extremely talented writer and producer on my own. Tim's life journey has many parallels which helped him understand the main theme of the book. God knew he was the best writer for my book! His patience with my never ending emails and letters and texts concerning additional information for the book entitles him to receive an "Honorary Serb" Award from me. (Drumroll) I think he needs a new name, Timothi Weeksić. Ha! I also heartily thank his devoted, lovely wife Teresa for introducing me to Tim!!!

My longtime, dear friend Elaine Millen for beautifully designing my website and this book.

The following clergy who inspired me to write the book: most especially Father Serafim Baltic, Abbott of New Gracanica Monastery who answered many of my numerous questions and emails and helped me realize a book like mine would be relevant and useful in today's world and needed to be written. Father Gregory Hohnholt of Holy Trinity Greek Orthodox Church for praying with Tim and me for the book's success before we began. Father Stephen Rogers of St. Ignatius Antiochian Orthodox Church for giving us his kind pastoral blessing as we finished the book. And Father Aleksandar Vujkovic of St. Petka Serbian Orthodox Church for his many kind and encouraging words.

I want to highlight my appreciation for Father Nektarios Serfes with the Decani Monastery Relief Fund, who opened my eyes to how important it is to serve our needy brothers and sisters in Christ. From malnourished children to desecrated churches, there is much we can do to minister to the physical and spiritual needs of God's people. Father Nektarios' life is an ongoing inspiration to me. In 2015, he received the prestigious St. Sava Medal from Serbian Orthodox Patriarch Irinej.

Finally my girlfriend iconographer Jennie Atty Gelles who is truly like a sister to me. Her loving words and encouragement kept me inspired to finish the book.

Thank you all for your love! I love each of you and May God bless each of you and keep you forever!

Ariane in her art studio with one of her completed paintings.

CHAPTER

I

GOD: THE FABRIC OF OUR LIVES

Samo Sloga Srbina Spasava: Only Unity Saves the Serbs

This is a famous quote by St. Sava, the first Archbishop and Enlightener of Serbia.

His purpose was to inspire his fellow Serbs to remain united to preserve their Orthodox Christian heritage and national identity.

Every word in the slogan begins with S, which is C in Cyrillic.

Thus, there are C's in every quadrant of the cross.

"Ask, and it shall be given you; seek, and ye shall find; knock, and it shall be opened unto you."
Matthew 7:7 (KJV)

My name is Ariane Michelle Trifunovic and I was born on December 1, 1963 in Wilmington, Delaware in the United States. Today, as Mrs. Anthony Montemuro, I'm a painter, a wife, and a mother of two beautiful children, living near Nashville, Tennessee. I'm blessed with God-given gifts as an artist, but I'm not a writer. But God asked me to write a book — my story of spiritual reawakening and discovery of the depth of my spiritual heritage as an Orthodox Christian.

My maiden name is a little different because I'm Serbian American. My family immigrated to the United States from the former Yugoslavia, a country in Eastern Europe. Trifunovic is even the "Americanized" spelling of the name; in Yugoslavia, our name included the accent, Trifunović, to indicate the ending pronunciation as "ch." So both spelling styles of Serbian names are included in my book. European names and locations include the accent; American versions do not. Some names, like my mother's maiden name, changed even more over time. Dobrić became Dobric, and some family members, such as my uncle Mike, started spelling it as Dobrich.

After the break-up of Yugoslavia, Serbia, where my family is from, became an independent country again. It's a land with a very rich Christian tradition as an Orthodox nation. Like Greece and Russia, Serbia has a long history with Orthodoxy, the second largest Christian Church in the world after Roman Catholicism. So, the Serbian Orthodox Church is the faith of my ancestors.

While my parents took me to church as a child, I didn't fully understand the services performed in the old Slavonic language, so like many others born into an "immigrant church," I took it for granted and spent most of my life not understanding or appreciating my Orthodox heritage. Only in recent years have I begun to experience the depth of faith found in Orthodox spirituality and it has changed me and brought so much joy into my life! Jesus tells us to "seek and we will find" and it's a journey worth sharing that will hopefully inspire you to find deeper meaning in your own walk as a Christian!

God is the fabric of our lives and that has special meaning for me. Nothing happens without a reason. God gave me a few threads to follow and they led me to a beautiful tapestry of Saints, prayer, and devotion. Now I live with God and His Holy Church as the center of all things in my life.

For me, it keeps coming back to my name and my family. We cannot escape our ancestral lineage and we're ultimately a product of our family; we also cannot escape God. The thread of family can ultimately lead us back to God, as well. We work out our salvation, or our journey to God, through our family and all the circumstances God allows to experience. So, I begin my story with my own family in order to share my journey to rediscovering the ancient Christian Orthodox faith of my parents and grandparents and great-grandparents. This faith laid the groundwork for me to hear Christ's call.

My Serbian Orthodox Christian parents were born in the former Yugoslavia — my mother Danica in Belgrade in 1932 and my father Aleksandar in Visegrad in 1923. My mother's Slava Saint was St. George until she got married, then it became St. Paraskeva, (or St. Petka as she is commonly known by Serbs) which I, in turn inherited. Her feast day is celebrated by the Serbian Orthodox Church on October 27th.

All Orthodox and Catholic Christians (and some Protestants) are familiar with namedays, the feast day on the liturgical calendar of the Saint for whom they were named. The Serbian Slava Saint is a bit different.

The Serbian family patron Saint Day or Krsna Slava is a Christian commemoration of the Saint on the day when the family ancestors were baptized. It is unique to the Serbian Orthodox Christian people and it's deeply instilled into their souls.

Once the Serbs became baptized Christians, they saw their family unit as a sanctified institution. St. Paul the Apostle teaches that the family is a "home church." In one of his letters, he says, "Greet Priscilla and Aquila my helpers in Christ Jesus... likewise greet the church that is in their house" (Romans 16:3, 5 KJV). St. John Chrysostom continued this theme when he called the family the "small church."

The Serbs began their history with the acceptance of Christianity and Holy Baptism and they did it freely and voluntarily because of the witness of Christian missionaries. This is the Ancient Christian faith which existed long before the beginning of Christian denominations. Christians, in general, celebrate Christmas in honor of Jesus' birth and Epiphany in remembrance of his baptism. These are examples of Christian feast or commemorative days. It's the same with the Serbian Krsna Slava; it is the most important day in the lives of our predecessors. Through baptism my ancestors became members of Christ's Church. Their patron Saint Day is their "spiritual birthday." In commemoration of their baptism, they began to celebrate Slava.

The first Archbishop, enlightener and unifier of Christian Serbia was St. Sava, a monk from Mt. Athos in Greece; he blessed and proclaimed Slava as a Christian institution. A ritual was prescribed to glorify God and venerate the family patron Saint. From then on, to be Serbian meant to celebrate Slava.[1]

St. Petka, my Slava Saint, is a very popular Serbian family patron Saint. She dressed poor people in her expensive clothes so she became the Patron Saint of such trades as spinning, sewing, weaving, and knitting. She was a fitting Saint for my father since he was a textile engineer who designed textile machine parts used to create a variety of fabrics. He had forty-eight patents registered with the Library of Congress in Washington, D.C. for his textile inventions.

It was a job offer at a textile firm called Bancroft in Wilmington, Delaware, that enabled him to immigrate to this country in 1955. My parents were married at St. Sava Serbian Orthodox Church in Northern Indiana, just outside of Chicago. The marriage sacrament was administered by the Very Rev. D.J. Shoukletovich, who also founded St. Nicholas, a Serbian church in Philadelphia, where I would be baptized and married years later.

I come from a distinguished Serbian family. My paternal grandfather, Ljubomir Trifunović, who passed away many years before my birth, was director of the Simović Lumber Mill in Yugoslavia and he served as Captain in the Royal Serbian Army during World War I. He would also serve his country again in World War II. My grandmother Vera was an amateur photographer.

I grew up knowing my maternal grandparents intimately. My maternal grandfather was Yugoslav Royal Army Artillery Lieutenant Colonel Velibor M. Dobrić, who attended Military Academy in Fountainbleau, France and served his country during World War II. My schoolteacher grandmother Darinka Kocić Dobrić was very proud that I was born on December 1, the date that Serbia joined with neighboring countries in 1918 to form the Kingdom of Serbs, Croats and Slovenes (later known as Yugoslavia) under the rule of the Serbian Karadjordjević dynasty. I have memories of my grandparents saying "Our Arianče" (my Serbian nickname) "was born on a very important date," like it was only fitting their first granddaughter would arrive on a day remembered by all Serbs. They took great care to impress our Serbian heritage on me, their next generation.

To be Serbian meant attending a Serbian Orthodox Church, of course. The church and Serbian people have a 1,500-year history dating back to the era of the Byzantine Empire. Even though we lived in Delaware when I was a child, my parents would make the trek to the closest Serbian church, St. Nicholas in Philadelphia, Pennsylvania, as often as it was practical. It was a 45-minute trip, but from my baptism until my twelfth birthday, this unassuming brick building in downtown Philly was our home church.

Since our church wasn't just around the corner, we didn't attend every Sunday. Vespers or extra services on weekdays were also out of the question with the exception of the major Christian feast days. The distance to church also gave me my first glimpse into other practices of Christianity. During the summer, my mother put me and my older brother Robert in a Presbyterian Church Vacation Bible School since it was closer to home. Looking back, I think it was her attempt to help us understand the Bible in English and there were no such summer schools at our little Philadelphia church. I remember vividly how exciting it was to learn about Joseph and his multicolored coat and drawing it on colored paper. I also recall seeing a movie about faraway places and Christian mission work which seemed exotic to my young eyes. I'm grateful that I went through this experience, because it helped me understand that the Bible was holy like the icons and everything else I observed as a child in the Serbian Church.

My understanding of the faith didn't come from any great intellectual knowledge. I faintly knew the Bible. I explored it very little on my own. I loved the Psalms, but got confused at the parts in the Gospels listing which ancestor begat who in the lineage of Christ. The Bible seemed long and confusing with no one there to encourage or guide me.

I was, however, quite familiar with how one should behave in church. I saw my parents kiss the Gospel book. On Sunday mornings, my dad typically wore a coat and tie, and my fashion-conscious mother was always "dressed to the nines." I saw how my parents respectfully crossed themselves and bowed their heads at different parts of the Liturgy and I, of course, learned to do the same. My Mama always bought candles in church for the living and the dead in our family, and she remembered long lists of names of our ancestors in prayer. I watched her as she lit each candle and kissed it prior to pressing it into the sand before the icons of Christ and the Virgin Mary.[2] So I observed how my parents treated everything in church with a deep reverence and holiness. That stayed with me throughout my life, and I never doubted that God existed because of what my parents taught me by example.

Mommy taught my brother and me "Oče Naš," which is the Lord's Prayer, as soon as we were able to memorize things. She taught us to memorize it in Serbian (the only way she knew it), and she impressed on us that it was a very important thing to know. Since I didn't know it in English, I didn't understand it was *the prayer* that Christ taught, however. I just knew that was what you said to God. The words were a bit complicated though because they weren't the everyday Serbian words I could comprehend. I recall in the 1970s there was a top ten hit on the radio that was basically "Our Father Who Art in Heaven" put to music and sung by Catholic nuns. As Mommy drove us around to all of our school activities in her light yellow Pontiac Lemans convertible, I would sing along, and that's how I learned to say the prayer in English and understand its meaning.

I remember the sounds and smells of church more than anything. All of my senses were engaged in church. I remember the richness, the beauty. Church felt ancient in every way. I never had to read anything to get that. The priest would swirl the censor, enveloping us in sweet incense smoke, and then he would dramatically disappear behind the Holy Doors of the Iconostasis and draw the curtains — it was all quite a mystery! It felt holy. The ceiling inside the church was blue with gold leaf stars that I would stare at endlessly and ponder where God was and what He was doing. Every inch of the walls was painted with holy scenes and figures. Since I didn't understand the Divine Liturgy in Old Slavonic, the imagery of the church captured my attention.

Communion was reserved for only several times a year, but I eagerly anticipated the holy bread the priest gave to everyone at the end of each liturgy, and we got really big pieces! Mommy always said, "It's the Ancient Church." I knew it was old without her telling me; I was a sensitive child. It felt old. It felt otherworldly — heavenly, actually. We even follow the old calendar, the Julian calendar, she told me. "We Pravoslavni (Serbian for Orthodox Christian) never change the holy traditions," she added.

Church for us Serbian Orthodox extended to our home as well. There was no division or separation between the church and the world. At home, my parents would find the Eastern wall, where the sun rises, to place our holy icons of Jesus, our Slava (family Patron) Saint, a cross, and Bogorodica, the Theotokos, the Ever-Virgin Mary. There was no explanation, it was just done. There was a space dedicated to God in our home — no questions asked. This was tradition and Serbs like tradition!

Tradition is what helped us preserve the Christian faith throughout the centuries. The Serbs really have no recorded history before their baptized history. God has always been the head of everything. Life centered on the Church and that was that. Our people suffered under the Muslim Turks for hundreds of years, while still remaining Christians. The Serbs are a stubborn, strong-willed people to their benefit. This trait helped them save the faith for future generations. As I look now, with older eyes, all Christians must be equally "stubborn" in order to preserve what we believe. We must put God first in each and every endeavor in our lives. We must fight to be a Christian. We must fight to preserve our faith and live God-centered lives, regardless of our nationality or ethnicity. Otherwise, a godless world will trample us and we'll lose the next generation.

Reaching the next generation — my children and yours — with the love of the traditions in our Holy Church is why God moved me to write this book. It's my story, but it's not about me. It's about God and the truth that we've been entrusted with, and it will die with us if we don't teach our faith to our children.

To be called by God to be His people means that we have a responsibility to preserve the truth and pass it down to our children and grandchildren for them to do the same. "I will make thy name to be remembered in all generations: therefore shall the people praise thee for ever and ever," says the psalmist in Psalm 45:17 (KJV). We must pray this prayer fervently every day.

If trends continue, Christians could become a minority in this country, and we Orthodox understand all too well what it's like being the minority of the minority for a long time, even though our church is growing in the United States. I came to understand as a teenager just how isolated one can be as an Orthodox Christian.

To be Serbian American as a child was somewhat confusing, in fact. There were maybe a handful of Serbs in Delaware where I grew up and then later, when we moved to North Carolina — virtually none. The small minority of Orthodox

Christians I came to know in North Carolina were Greeks. Orthodox churches in those days were virtually all ethnic, founded by immigrants to retain their culture and religion. I never knew the Divine Liturgy could be celebrated in English. How things have changed. Now there is Ancient Faith Radio. There is Light and Life Publishing and Ancient Faith Publishing. Back then it was difficult even finding a simple book on Orthodox Christianity.

The Holy Traditions and oral traditions — especially Slava — are what kept the faith for so many of us who were sons and daughters of immigrants. Nowadays parents have many resources available at their fingertips about the Orthodox Christian faith and ways to teach their kids. In my time, there was none of this; the church and its rituals were all I had in addition to observing my parents. There was no one like me in school. My Easter was at different times than others and my religious Christmas (or Božić) was on January 7. We didn't live in a Serbian community. Even so, my parents diligently upheld the Church traditions.

My parents, who left Yugoslavia in the 1950s to come to the Unites States, viewed themselves as émigrés rather than immigrants since they came here for political rather than economic reasons. They also came here speaking English and many other languages. They were educated and skilled. I never once heard them refer to themselves as immigrants. My father came here due to a job offer. Instead of being part of an established Serbian neighborhood in Wilmington, my father's work actually blended us into a global community. His friends through work included American, Swiss, Dutch, Japanese and a variety of other nationalities. My parents saw themselves as international citizens and it was reflected in their social lives. My mother spoke French and Russian and my father spoke fluent German and Dutch. Additionally, both spoke perfect English and Serbian. We were Europeans living in America. We were from Yugoslavia and then within Yugoslavia, we were Serbian. The Trifunovic family was a tapestry of old and new world and my parents were quite at ease in their new life in America!

I remember travelling to Europe for the first time at age seven; we visited many countries, and in each one either my mother or my father would take over speaking and translating. Finally, we arrived at Heathrow Airport in London and I asked, "Ok which language do they speak here? Who knows British?" Dad responded, "You know this language, little one." I gave him a perplexed look and wondered what language this could be? I was really confused as my dad just grinned.

My parents were an impressive couple together. My father was a tall man. He was 6'2" and I remember his large hands were matched with a gentle spirit, sense of humor, and refined aura. He was sensitive, intelligent, and a true European gentleman. Aleksandar Trifunovic was warm and loving to all people and that always stood out to me. He would always stand when a lady entered the room.

Daddy opened doors for Mommy and even stood when she went to the restroom when we dined at a restaurant.

He loved anything to do with home and family life. Mama never used a repairman for anything in twenty-three years of marriage. Daddy was the guy! He could fix anything! He was the quintessential engineer-minded repairman. He was quite the chef too. He enjoyed grilling steaks, baking bread, and making Serbian sarma or stuffed cabbage.

Daddy's hobby, though, was making things out of metal; he was a metalsmith with a studio in the garage. You name it and he made it, from frames and tables to easels and jewelry boxes. Even towards the end of his short life, he fashioned a three-bar Orthodox cross out of brass. It laid on his chest at his funeral and it was used by the priests at my wedding and the baptisms of six grandchildren. He never knew these beautiful grandchildren, but his cross was there for them. It is still curious to me that he had this urge to make a cross just before his sudden and unexpected death.

Daddy first saw my beautiful mother around 1957 while he was on a textile business trip to Paris, France, where Mama was majoring in linguistics at Sorbonne University. Mama was waiting for her visa to be completed to the United States. She was staying at the home of French General Besançon, a friend of her father's. To earn extra money, she was a nanny to an American family and she also modeled hats for (haute couture) fashion designer Nina Ricci. It was at one of Nina's fashion shows that my father first noticed Danica Velibor Dobrić. Seated next to Ricci, his eyes lit up as Mama walked down the runway. Nina poked him and said, "Alex, the one who catches your eye is from your country of Yugoslavia!" Dad never forgot that.

For better or worse, my mother is an unforgettable personality. At her best, she is elegant, beautiful, warm, funny, and intelligent. At her worst, pride can get in her way and make her bitter. In all cases, Mama is never dull.

As a younger woman, she was a classic beauty with perfectly applied lipstick and nail color. She attended several years of medical school in Belgrade before her father called for her to leave Yugoslavia as the new communist government tightened its grip in the years after World War II. She left a serious boyfriend and bright medical career behind and obeyed her parents' wishes. The last of her family to escape, she followed her father's path to the U.S. through Paris. She often tells the frightful story of abruptly leaving her life behind — unable to tell her friends for fear they may betray her escape. She boarded the Orient Express train with her aunt, who was a pediatrician and Mama's inspiration. While on the train, she was so scared that she became ghostly pale; her aunt told her to put blush on her face so she wouldn't look so sickly — or guilty.

Mama willingly left Yugoslavia so the family could be reunited in America. Her father had left years earlier and was unable to return to a communist nation, so he had not seen his wife and children in seventeen years! Mama recalls a gray-haired man waving his arms on the railroad tracks of Chicago when she arrived. She didn't even recognize her dear father, whom she hadn't seen since she was eight years old!

Mama's presence was always big, and it still is, even today. She can still change languages with ease. Everything in life she learned through its many changes and she always found uses for her talents. When my brother and I were younger, she put her linguistic skills to work as a French teacher to schoolchildren and an interpreter for executives at DuPont.

Later, when we lived in North Carolina, her fashion experience in Paris and life with a textile engineer led her to open a fashion consulting business, DVT Enterprises International. She taught Southern women how to dress high style, like the ladies in New York and Paris! My mother's roommate in France, Annick Bickert, said she could always make something out of nothing. With just a few scarves, a skirt or two, and a blouse, Mama could create a million outfits!

Mommy was also very big on high heels and gold jewelry. Once on our way to church, she made Daddy go back home because she forgot her jewelry. When she got back in the car, he asked, "Do you have your artillery on now?" Mama smiled, "Sure-da-yeh!" which was a combination of English and Serbian they liked to exchange with each other. They were like an "Old World" European couple living in America. Everything was understated classic elegance.

My parents never complained about anything either, and I admired that quality. They left everything behind in Communist Yugoslavia and even though they were isolated from their language and culture, they were happy to move on and build a new life and raise children. They were taught that attitude by example by my grandfather Velibor Dobrić, the artillery colonel. He refused two offers that would have continued his military career. One was with the French Foreign Legion, which could have ultimately led to the rank of Brigadier General. The alternative was to return to Sarajevo and teach ballistics in the new order established by Communist strongman Josip Broz Tito. He rejected these offers because he had sworn an oath to serve a Christian king, Aleksandar I (who was assassinated in 1934) in the Yugoslav Royal Army. He couldn't serve a communist and atheist leader so he knew his time in uniform was over. Instead, this Serbian and French trained officer was willing to work as a common laborer in a U.S. steel mill near Chicago to start a new life in a free country. He was a model of perseverance. Life never beat him down. I remember how he would go for walks when he visited us in Delaware. He walked erect with his hands folded in the small of his back — always the 'Colonel.'

A year before he died, when I was ten years old, I was cast as an angel and soldier in "The Nutcracker" at the Wilmington Playhouse. He got to see his granddaughter roll out the cannon in a ballet. He was so proud he jumped up to clap and shout "Bravo Ariance!"

Time is now changing my family into memories. My grandfather passed away in 1974. My dad died of a heart attack in 1982. And my beautiful mother is now in need of nursing care with dementia. It's up to me to tell their stories, or they will all be forgotten.

The children and grandchildren of immigrants to America are more and more American and less of their original ethnic heritage. I guess that's why the U.S. is called the "melting pot." We all stand together as Americans regardless of color or ethnicity. But in recent years, it has become more important to reclaim my Serbian heritage because of the Christian faith they fought so dearly to preserve.

In the story to come, you will see the rich tapestry that Orthodoxy is to my family. It truly is the fabric of my life. I'm reminded of this daily by a Serbian Coat of Arms tapestry that now hangs in my home; it was given to my grandfather in the early 1960s by King Peter II, Yugoslavia's king in exile and the son of King Aleksandar. It was given to him at a prestigious event in northern Indiana, and my grandfather sat at the head table with King Peter.

The metaphors for tapestry in my life are unavoidable. My father broke with tradition to name me Ariane. Instead of following the Serbian tradition of naming children after their paternal grandparents, he preferred new names. He learned of the name Ariane in his twenties while attending the Hogere Textile School in Enschede, in the Netherlands, and was inspired by a statue of Ariadne he saw while living there. She was a Greek goddess, the daughter of Minos and Mistress of the Labyrinth. The name Ariadne, or Ariane, means "Very Holy Maid." She saved her lover Theseus, who slew the Minotaur, from being lost in the labyrinth, or maze, by providing him with a golden thread to follow to find his way out. She became a symbol or a mascot of the textile school with the "thread" connection. There are many derivations of this name — Ariana, or Arianna or Ariadna. My father chose Ariane.

Something told my dad that I was a girl even before I was born. He sat my mother down while she was pregnant and told her I had to be named Ariane. Why? My Mom thought it was too difficult a name with Trifunovic as a last name, but he was quite persistent and he wouldn't budge, which wasn't typical of his personality.

So by fate or destiny or simply my father's strong will, here I am, Ariane Trifunovic Montemuro — the daughter of a Serbian textile engineer, in search of what it means to be Serbian…and Orthodox.

Great men and women of God have strengthened and fortified my journey. After a series of miraculous events in my early forties, I embarked on a thorough study of the ancient Orthodox Christian faith; one favorite Russian Holy Elder I discovered was Elder Barsanuphius of Optina Monastery (1845-1913). His Christ-centered words opened my eyes to deeply examine my faith, my life, and my family.

In his biography, he reminds us to spiritually interpret our lives down to the minutest details. "Our whole life is a great mystery of God," he said. "All of life's circumstances, no matter how insignificant they seem, have enormous meaning. We will understand the meaning of the present life in the future age. How circumspectly we need to regard it, but we leaf through our life like a book, page after page, not being aware of what is written in it. There is nothing accidental in life; all is done according to the will of the Creator. May the Lord vouchsafe us in this life to acquire the right to enter into eternal life."[3]

Elder Barsanuphius inspired me to dig into the past to know the circumstances that brought me to this point in my journey. This great Holy Elder also said that names can have special meanings. In the Bible, almost every name means something. Eve means "life," since she became the mother of all humanity. God commanded Abram to change his name to Abraham since he would be a father of many nations (Genesis 17:5). And his wife Sarai, "my lady" became Sarah, "the lady of a multitude."[4]

With a name like Ariane, a name that had special meaning to my father, I often ponder the meaning of these words as they apply to my life — and soon, you will too.

CHAPTER

II

TAPESTRY OF CHILDHOOD MEMORIES

"And Jacob went out from Beersheba, and went toward Haran. And he lighted upon a certain place, and tarried there all night, because the sun was set; and he took of the stones of that place, and put them for his pillows, and lay down in that place to sleep. And he dreamed, and behold a ladder set up on the earth, and the top of it reached to heaven: and behold the angels of God ascending and descending on it.... And Jacob awaked out of his sleep, and he said, Surely the Lord is in this place; and I knew it not. And he was afraid, and said, How dreadful is this place! this is none other but the house of God, and this is the gate of heaven."

Genesis 28: 10-12; 16-17 (KJV)

Aside from my birth date, the most important day of my life occurred on January 12, 1964. This was my baptismal day, or Krštenje in Serbian. My grandfather held the censer for the Serbian priest, Father, or Prota, Very Reverend Živan Gavrilović. As I pointed out earlier, our Serbian church was forty-five minutes away from our home and I was just six weeks old. My mother was probably worried about driving such a tiny baby so far in the frigid dead of winter, so she opted for the home baptism. Her parents were there, as well as her brother, and she made a lovely meal for all who came. It was a great day for my parents. First they had a son and now a daughter and both were baptized into their ancestral faith...the same Serbian Orthodox faith that had withstood so many opposing forces including many centuries under the oppression of the Ottoman Empire. And now, both children were born and baptized in their new American country.

It was a significant moment in our family's history also because it brought us together to carry on our faith and tradition. My grandfather had left home to defend Yugoslavia in World War II when Mommy was eight years old. He was captured and sent to an officer's prisoner-of-war camp in Germany. After the war, he immigrated to the United States and never returned to Yugoslavia. A total of seventeen years passed before my mother would see him again when she stepped off that train in Chicago in 1958, and the family was finally reunited. Now, many years later, my grandparents and my uncle were together with us again to share in my baptism. As the priest baptized me, my military-minded grandfather stood at attention with the censer, which symbolized our prayers rising to heaven.[1]

My baptism also came during an important period in our lives as Serbian Orthodox Christians. Christmas, or Božić, is celebrated on January 7 and Theophany, or Bogojavljenje, the feast day for Christ's baptism, is celebrated on January 19, after which Orthodox priests begin blessing the homes of the faithful with holy water. Theophany, or Epiphany, as it is known in the West, means "the revelation of God" and the Serbian word is the literal translation of the Greek. My baptism fell in between these two holy days on the Serbian Orthodox Calendar. It was a time when Serbs also looked forward to January 27, the feast day for St. Sava, the Archbishop of Serbia, one of the most important Saints to our people.

I recently discovered that January 12 also has special meaning to the Serbian people. On that day, an icon of the Virgin Mary, known as the Akathist icon, is commemorated. The icon of our Holy Mother miraculously survived a fire in 1837 at Hilandar, the Serbian monastery founded by St. Sava at Mt. Athos in Greece.

My baptism was the beginning of a very special relationship with my grandfather. My Deka, as we called him in Serbian, delighted in his new role. After missing seventeen years of parenting his own son Mihailo and daughter (my mother) Danica due to the political upheavals in Yugoslavia, he was ready to enjoy being a Deka (grandfather)! God graciously bestowed upon him two grandchildren — grandson Robert, who he called Robbie or Robica, and the granddaughter, Ariane or Arianče. In addition, another granddaughter, my cousin Doris, or Doja as we call her, was born several years after his death.

Deka gave us all the love he could to make up for not being a father to his own children. He enjoyed being silly and making facial grimaces and little noises to make us kids laugh. My grandfather passed his silly gestures to his son Mike, who still to this day loves to kid around and make jokes for a laugh. My Uncle Mike has my Deka's silly gene!

More importantly though, Grandfather paid close attention to us and tried to foster our God-given gifts and talents. Deka saw me as an artist, and he always gave me art supplies as presents, even when I was very young. They weren't kid's art supplies, but adult, high-quality, professional-grade art materials. He gave me a case of paints and hand painted my name, ARIANE TRIFUNOVIC, in beautiful white script in Latin letters and then next to it in Cyrillic, Ариане Трифуновић.

In addition to his job at U.S. Steel, my grandfather had a sign painting business on the side in Gary, Indiana, and he would often be paid in cash for his signs. When he would visit, he would shove $500 in my mom's hand "for the grandchildren," and it would always make her mad. She did not want his generosity, and back in the 1960s that was a lot of money as cash! Mommy just wanted him to visit. She wanted to be near him. Deka, however, was showing us how much he loved us.

Love is what I remember most about my family during this time. My dad and grandfather would talk about the old country and laugh together a lot. Dad would affectionately call him Ćale, or Pop. I could tell even as a young girl that Deka approved of him for his daughter. Of all the things Deka talked about though, he never talked about his painful past — his incarceration in a German POW camp when he lost so much weight or the painful decision he made to leave his family behind when he immigrated to America to start a new life at the age of fifty-one. He always focused on the future. My uncle recently told me his best trait was perseverance. I can see that now. But what did I see then? I just saw a grandfather loving me. He was a silly grandfather sipping Christian Brothers brandy when it was time to unwind.

Visiting us the fall before his death, he came to me after a long walk and said, "Arianče, I have a surprise for you!" I thought it was a doll or a toy, but then from behind his back he revealed a great big, multi-colored fall leaf. Then he proudly said, "I knew you especially would love this!" I graciously, but half-heartedly accepted the leaf, but it was not until after his death that I began to understand this unusual gift and how he knew me so deeply before I even knew myself.

One day, it all changed so quickly. The phone rang. Deka had been taken to Saint Catherine's Hospital outside of Chicago where they kept him overnight for observation. Then came a fatal heart attack and that was it. He was gone at seventy-four.

I remember more phone calls and the confusion. It was my first experience of death. I wasn't sure what to expect, and at age eleven I wasn't mature enough to understand exactly what was going on. I had never been to a funeral. Mommy packed and Daddy loaded up the car, and we planned the long trip from Delaware to northern Indiana. We went to bed early to prepare for the long drive ahead.

I fell fast asleep as I usually do…only to awake in the middle of the night to see my newly deceased grandfather sitting on the edge of my bed! "Hi Ariančе!" He looked just as he did in life. "Hi, Deka!" I responded. Then we suddenly left my bedroom and found a seat outside on the backyard garden bench made by my dad. He just looked me in the eye and spoke without moving his lips and said, "You should see it up there, Ariančе; you, of all people, would love the colors. You won't even believe the colors! Do you want to come?" I looked at him and I thought — Deka wants me to come to heaven and he just died! Does that mean I will die? I can't die and leave Mommy, Daddy and Robbie! Well, it was as if he read my thoughts and saw my fear and he said, "No worries, it's okay!"

Then we returned to my room and he tucked me gently back into my bed and he left. The dream was so vivid, so real that all these years later as I write this, I can see it in my mind's eye clearly. It was not like any dream I have ever had. It was so real. It was super real. I believe my grandfather visited me that night.

The next day, the drive to Indiana seemed endless. We arrived and I saw for the first time a lifeless person before me — someone I had known intimately. I leaned over to kiss my deceased grandfather on the forehead, and everything came together for me in an instant — the gift of the leaf and the dream. My grandfather knew I loved beauty. He knew I would love the leaf because I loved color! He told me to come with him to heaven so I could see the unbelievable colors there too. He wanted to show me because he knew I would understand. He could not contain his excitement about his heavenly abode and he wanted to share it with me. With this revelation, I started to cry. I realized he was really gone, and he was in heaven with God. He showed me through the dream.

My Deka's death was the beginning of many changes in our family. In 1975, as I turned eleven years old, recession gripped the nation and my father lost his job in Wilmington after twenty years due to a corporate buyout and restructuring. My dad started working abroad and considered moving to Holland or Geneva, Switzerland, but my parents really didn't want to go back to Europe.

Finally, Daddy found the right opportunity in Burlington, North Carolina. It was a small town, but my father really liked the company and especially its CEO, Roger Gant. He was a mutual friend of my dad's closest buddy and classmate from

Yugoslavia, Paul DeMarsano. So in the summer of 1975, we packed up and headed south. I asked Daddy if there were palm trees in North Carolina and he laughed and said, "No, not quite, Ariančě."

My parents found a lovely all-brick colonial home in Burlington and suddenly we were Serbian transplants in the middle of the Deep South. I'm pretty sure we were the only Serbs there. How do you say "howdy, y'all" with a Serbian accent? We adapted and came to love the slower pace of life in North Carolina. The cost of living was far more reasonable than Delaware, as well.

There was a small Orthodox community, but it was Greek. There were a few Greek families in the area and a small Greek Orthodox Church, St. Katherine, which we began to attend. The church didn't have services every Sunday because the priest was an engineer from Raleigh and he commuted to Burlington whenever he could. But this became our new church home and I started hearing Greek, instead of Old Slavonic, during Liturgy.

It was also during this time that I discovered my new love for ballet and we began to look for a school I could attend. My new mentor and inspiration was Russian prima ballerina Anna Pavlova (1881-1931). I discovered her in an old dusty book in the downtown Burlington library. Opening the book of black and white photos, I was so moved by all the beauty I saw. She moved me in ways I could not have imagined before.

Anna was like me; she was different. She was also an Orthodox Christian! I read how she crossed herself [2] before every performance. She loved the Mother of God, the Virgin Mary, and once designed a dance in honor of her. In her, I found a friend; I found someone I could relate to in a place where I felt very alone.

She was elegant. The way she dressed and carried herself exuded grace in every detail. I poured over pictures of her for hours on end. Her eyes and the beauty of her soul radiated in every picture.

Anna was unique in other ways too. She gave her life to her art. She was modest, and she even danced in a circus tent when the theatre was unavailable just so she could share her beauty with the people she loved so much.

A native of St. Petersburg, Anna loved her country and the Russian people. She supported Serbian orphans after World War I. She loved all animals, but swans in particular. I was mesmerized by her — an artist with such a big heart. I fell in love with her and Anna's Russian culture. Many people don't realize it was Anna Pavlova that introduced ballet to the United States.

I did make friends in Burlington, of course, but none of them were like me and my new mentor. At a deeper level, even though I was only twelve at the time, I think I was searching for a more meaningful connection to my Orthodox faith. I wanted to know more, and Anna offered a striking pose for how an Orthodox Christian should live their life.

I believe every human has a yearning for God. We all ultimately search for Him even when we don't realize it, outwardly at least. For me, Anna Pavlova demonstrated so many Christian virtues. She believed there was beauty in all things, in words and deeds, and beauty helped humanity grow and flourish. My young, artistic soul wanted to relate to Anna's vision of life.

Daddy and Mommy were amazed that I found such inspiration in a Russian Orthodox woman. For me, it began a great love affair with Russia that continues to this day. Even as a young girl, I dreamed that if I ever became a mother to a little girl, I would name her Anna. That dream came true and my daughter is Ana, however, with only one "n" in her name.

So with Anna Pavlova as my new role model, off I went to pursue my dream of becoming a ballerina. I went to ballet summer school twice, and in ninth grade, I attended a ballet boarding school, the North Carolina School for the Performing Arts. My parents were supportive, but Mommy hesitated when it sunk in that I was actually leaving home at age thirteen. Daddy said to her, "Žabac (Serbian for frog as a nickname since my mother liked frogs), you better let her go so she has no regrets when she is thirty years old."

Parents can be protective of their children, but sometimes they can be overprotective out of fear. In my teen years, I began to understand more about the fearfulness that comes with Serbian superstitions and intuitions.

I knew that we were a Christian family even though issues of faith were not openly discussed. As I explained in Chapter 1, the practice of the faith was all I ever experienced. Our faith was something that was never questioned. But when something bad happened, Mommy sometimes explained it might be a punishment from God and only God knew. Whenever there was a worry in life she would go to church and light a candle!

But many people of Serbian and Balkan heritage have inherited a culture of superstitions to explain the unknowns of life. They analyze dreams and read the remains of Turkish coffee grounds to foretell the future. Or dropping a knife or spoon can have some important meaning.

One of my mom's most common beliefs is "dancing eyes." A twitching left eye means you have bad news ahead; the right eye brings good news. If you scratch your left palm, money is coming your way, but if it's your right hand, you will be losing money or paying it out.

These so-called superstitions are different, though, from fortune-telling. Many countries like Serbia and Greece, which have been immersed in the Orthodox Christian faith for so long, have developed a symbolic language to discern the presence of good or evil. This is not something a person seeks out. It's just a natural way of feeling the presence of the Holy Spirit or not. This is something that many Serbs "feel" and it's not the same thing as dabbling in psychic phenomena, which was to become my future sin; I didn't understand the distinction at the time.

The reading of coffee grounds does fall into the fortune telling category, however, and it shouldn't be practiced or sought out. It is so common-place among Serbs that I recall a lady in the Hancock Street church in Philadelphia turning her Turkish coffee cup over and reading the grounds for herself and others after Liturgy in fellowship hall. No one thought anything of it, but had we known the Bible, we would have understood that searching for the future in this way can lead us away from God. We are to trust God for our future and seek it in prayer and not look for shortcuts in superstitions. I learned this many years later.

My mother was never interested in people reading Turkish coffee grounds. She didn't understand why people were so interested in the future. God gives what he gives. It's not up to us to question these things.

She was more interested in the past and discussing her heritage — her people, her ancestors. Mama's list for the living and the dead to commemorate in prayer went back several generations and she never forgot anyone. When I got married, she added my husband and his family and so on.

I, on the other hand, have always been interested in the future. Even as a child, it intrigued me, especially if it was attached to dreams. Ever since I dreamed of my deceased grandfather, my life has been one of vivid and often symbolic dreaming.

Dreams and visions can have great meaning. My mother recalled a man stopping her in Belgrade when she was a pre-teen, on her way home from school. He predicted she would go across a big ocean one day and marry a man much older than her, and she would have a son and then a daughter. He wanted to tell her more, but she got scared and ran away since her Baka (grandmother) told her to never speak to strangers. She remembered the incident after she gave birth to me.

This story stuck in my childish mind because I wished my mom did not run away! I wanted to know more! I was curious. What would happen next? I was intrigued, and I wanted to know the future and the possibilities it held for me.

When I was almost eighteen, Mommy, or Mamica as I liked to call her, had her own feeling about the future. Her left eye began to dance — not a little, but a lot, so something really bad was about to happen. When I came home from college, she repeated her worry to me and my brother. To us, it was just normal. This was just her personality, a trait passed down to her by her mother and grandmother.

Shortly after her left eye started dancing, we took a trip to South Carolina to furnish our new oceanfront condo in Garden City. We hauled a round redwood table with four benches on the roof of Daddy's Oldsmobile station wagon. Along the way, we heard a huge crash and boom. We got out of the car and Mommy put her hands on her hips and said in Serbian, "Oh no…this is not good; something bad is going to happen." She saw that out of four benches, one fell off and was smashed to pieces, leaving only three. Less than two weeks later, my father had a massive heart attack, and our family of four was reduced to three.

So what are we to make of Mommy's intuition? This was not a New Age thing. Was it her way of interpreting a symbolic language where the Holy Spirit could warn her of impending attacks of evil?

These are deep issues of spiritual discernment and as I became an adult, I was not mature enough as a Christian to know these things. My curiosity would lead me down the wrong paths and away from God. But from childhood, the weaving of the tapestry of dreams and intuitions had begun in my life and it would eventually bring me full circle back into the arms of the Orthodox Church.

SCRAPBOOK MEMORIES

I

My Serbian Roots…

*The remains of Serbian men massacred by Bulgarian soldiers
in the town of Surdulica.*

~

*Ariane's great-grandfather, Very Reverend Trandafil Kocić, was one of the very
first victims of this mass murder of Serbia's finest men, 1915.*

Wedding of Ariane's maternal grandparents,
Darinka Kocić and Colonel Velibor Dobrić, 1931.

The Dobrić Family, pre-World War II. Ariane's young mother Danica is in center.

The Dobrić family seeing Velibor off to battle in World War II, Yugoslavia, April 1941.

Ariane's mother Danica and Uncle Mihailo.

The Dobrić family during World War II.

Ariane's maternal great-grandfather, a book translator and writer, Mihailo Dobrić (with mustache); his first grandchild, Ariane's mother, Danica Velibor Dobrić is seated far right.

Vera Skrober Trifunović, Ariane's "mysterious" and artsy paternal grandmother.

Ariane's paternal grandfather, Ljubomir, as young boy (right) in traditional Serbian costume.

*Ariane's grandfather, Captain Ljubomir Trifunović
(lower right in leather boots) during World War I.*

*Ariane's paternal grandmother (standing) and great-grandmother (seated)
scrying to see their future by divination.*

Ariane's father, Aleksandar, as a child celebrating Slava St. Petka with both sets of grandparents, 1929.

*Ariane's maternal great-grandmother, Natalia Popović Kocić, who came from a priestly family.
Her father was an Orthodox priest from Kragujevac. Her uncle on her father's side was
Bishop Domentijan of Niš. Her husband, Very Reverend Trandafil Kocić,
served the Orthodox Church in Leskovac, Serbia.*

*The sad day in Belgrade that Ariane's grandmother (shown in white scarf) said goodbye
to her family while en route to America.
Darinka Kocić Dobrić would never see her mother Natalia again.*

CHAPTER

III

SEEK GOD FIRST
AND HIS WILL (NOT YOURS) FOR YOUR LIFE

"…for your heavenly Father knoweth that ye have need of all these things. But seek ye first the kingdom of God, and his righteousness; and all these things shall be added unto you."

Matthew 6:32-33 (KJV)

If you could know the future, would you? Some would say yes, because you could pick the right investments and be rich. Others might hesitate. What if you knew tomorrow was your last day on Earth?

To be human is to be curious, but too much curiosity can lead to sin. In fact, that was the original sin of Adam and Eve. The serpent told them if they ate of the fruit, they would know all things just like God. The Lord knows all things, so it sounded like a pretty good deal, but it led to our separation from God and death (Genesis 3:1-21).

Dabbling into the unknown didn't end there, of course. The Old Testament is full of scripture where God forbids his chosen people, the Hebrews, from contacting the dead or practicing any form of divination.[1] The church retained this moral code in its teachings and it has fought a 2,000-year battle with witchcraft, sorcery, devil worship, and some of the less threatening forms that we know today as New Age practices.

Christians who are not well grounded in the faith can fall into these spiritual side-roads and practice both without realizing the dangers. It can be confusing because every culture passes down forms of superstitions. The Serbs, like other Europeans, have their healthy share, such as my mother's many superstitions described in the previous chapter. Some could be described as a gift or spiritual insight, however. Mommy didn't seek her dreams or visions; *they came to her.*

Seeking out the future or spirits is where we can get into trouble. Looking back today, it bothers me that some Serbian people engaged in reading Turkish coffee grounds after church. Maybe they considered it "entertainment," but this was going on after the Divine Liturgy on church property! At Venice Beach, California, astrologers and fortune tellers line the sidewalks like some sort of occult fair, ready to tell you what the future holds. Imagine if these people were in your fellowship hall after church!

Maybe these things can be genetic as well. My paternal grandmother, Vera Skrober Trifunović, was of Slovenian ancestry. She was an artist and amateur photographer and she had an air of mystery about her. She converted to Orthodoxy from Catholicism to marry my grandfather Ljubomir, but she always crossed herself as Catholics do,[2] so maybe she remained a Catholic at heart in some ways.

But Grandmother Trifunović also dabbled in "the arts." I have a rare picture of her with her mother looking into a bowl of water — a form of divination called "scrying." Like Turkish coffee grounds, scrying is another way to interpret the future. One can see future events in the stirring of the waters. She also had a psychic mid-wife with her when my father was born. She told my grandmother she would have two sons, one who would achieve fame in his field (my father and his many textile patents) and another son who would become wealthy (my uncle Sinisha or Sid).

So my Slovenian grandmother was very interested in the future, and she found ways other than praying for God's will to satisfy her curiosity. I think I inherited that same curiosity. I had the "gift" like my mother, with the dream of my departed maternal grandfather serving as an example, but as a young woman, I wanted to know more.

My weakness as a "cradle Orthodox" was that I was familiar with Christian rituals, but I didn't know our faith very well. I knew about God, but I didn't really know Him. Even in my twenties and thirties, I still didn't possess a detailed knowledge of God. I believed in Him and I also loved the Bogorodica or Theotokos, the Mother of our Lord Jesus Christ, but I didn't grasp what it meant to work at being a Christian. Salvation (as I understand now) is a lifelong process; it doesn't happen instantaneously. Our faith in Christ has the power to change lives and as Christians, we're challenged to become spiritual athletes — not just to know him, but to participate or live in him. How do we live in him? We do so by praying persistently. Prayer is how we spiritually contact God. We also fast to suppress the needs of the physical body so we may keep our eye on the prize — Christ. Fasting reminds us that this earthly life is a temporary passage to our soul's true home when we leave our bodies behind. We go to church as much as possible and repent and receive communion. We participate in the sacraments to be spiritually nourished and continue our race to Christ. Our lives must continually revolve around Christ and the Church. Our life in Christ must be purposeful and devout. Abiding in him, he can mold us and continually renew our lives.

As a kid, what I got was bits and pieces of who God was and how to worship Him. I knew my faith was ancient and beautiful and that spoke to me. I knew I had to preserve it for future generations. But that's about it. I knew I had to cross myself and pray and fast, but I didn't have the big picture where God was at the helm of everything. That part was fuzzy for me. I knew God was out there as the Creator of everything, but I did not see Him as the center of my life yet.

I was no wild child growing up. I was a good young girl and a good young lady. I never tried drugs. I told boys I dated that I would not say "I love you" because I was saving that for my future husband. My mother didn't tell me to say that. It was just understood I would be a certain way as a Christian woman. My faith preserved me in many ways even in my ignorance! There was an inherent goodness that was part of my very being.

Even though there was an inherent goodness about me, my curiosity would become my vice and addiction. I was fascinated with the hidden language of life — the intuitive world. But I didn't understand the difference between the intuitive world that includes God and the other world that doesn't. I became confused when I opened my mind to New Age practices as a young adult.

The drift began when I started college. Ballet had been my life through boarding school, and art remained my passion as I finished high school back home in North Carolina. I even won some state and national art awards! College, at first, was a private school, Meredith College in Raleigh, but my freshman year was interrupted by my father's sudden death.

Daddy worked for a private company that didn't have a pension plan, so his death forced our family into some difficult financial decisions. My brother Robert was in medical school at East Carolina University in Greenville so my mother decided it would be more affordable if I attended a state college and lived with him. It turned out to be a good move since ECU had a respected art department. I graduated cum laude with a degree in art history the same day my brother graduated from medical school.

The down side to college life is that I didn't seek out an Orthodox Church to continue practicing my faith. The fact that Orthodox churches were hard to find in the South was a convenient excuse. When we travelled as a family, Mommy would always look for a church so she could light a candle and say her prayers for the living and the dead. I departed from that example and lived like a lot of other college kids who don't make church a priority when they're on their own.

After college, our time in North Carolina came to an end. Robbie started his residency in Philadelphia, and I enrolled in the master's program at George Washington University in Washington, D.C., hoping for a career in a museum one day. Mother sold our home in North Carolina and bought a house in Elkins Park, a suburb of Philly, and my brother moved in with her. After finishing my master's, I joined them and worked several museum and art gallery jobs in the Philadelphia area.

It was during this time that I became an avid reader. I read about well-known artists and their philosophical beliefs, and I myself began exploring the meaning of life. I was searching for a mentor artist like I had with Anna Pavlova when I was a young girl. I could not find one. What I found were mainly artists like Walt Whitman and Wassily Kandinsky who wrote about their very unique metaphysical beliefs, including spiritualism and reincarnation. I began to ask many questions. Is there such a thing as fate? Why do some people die young and others do not? Why are some people born a certain way and others not? Why was I here now? As I searched deeply, I didn't have a proper spiritual father to guide me, and I attended church infrequently. I muddled through by myself, never putting God into my equations.

With his residency over, Robert decided to move to California, and he wanted all of us to follow him. I really didn't want to go, but I applied for a job at the San Diego Museum of Art where I thought I had a foot in the door. Then on New Year's Eve 1988, I was told the position was no longer available. I began to feel very down, and I decided I wanted to be married and have a more stable life.

To find a husband, I turned to the God I had been ignoring and started praying, "If you're really there, help me get married." Then I had the audacity to give God my long list of qualifications. "Dear God, please bring me the following type of man…"

1. A man who loves the arts
2. A man who wants to have children
3. A man older than me
4. A man with glasses (I guess because Daddy wore them)
5. A man who wants our kids to go to college
6. A loyal man that would never cheat on me
7. A man that was not too tall — I did not want to look way up to him
8. A man that was a professional
9. A Serbian or Greek or Russian or Romanian American (I tried to think of all the Orthodox compatible guys)
10. But then about 4 weeks into the prayer, I thought I better give God more options and since Italians have expressive temperaments like Serbs, I added Italian American — as long as he would allow me to raise our children Orthodox and be married in an Orthodox Church

I even ended the prayer in Jesus' name at the urging of one of my girlfriends. I put the prayer in a Bible and every night before bed for the next eight weeks, I prayed fervently. And in February, 1989, God answered. A family that knew my brother at Temple University Hospital came to our home to look at fur and leather coats that my mother had designed. Dr. John Fitzgerald, who was a chief resident there, wanted to buy one for his wife, Georgia. During their fashion appointment with Mommy, John's grandmother latched on to me and suggested I go out with another grandson, Tony Montemuro. John and Georgia then arranged a blind date and within eight weeks of praying that prayer, an Italian-American doctor walked through our front door to become my fiancé and future husband. In the depths of my unhappiness, God heard my prayer!

Tony and I were married at our old family church, St. Nicholas Serbian Orthodox Church in Philadelphia, on November 17, 1990. This was the same church founded by the priest who married my parents; the cornerstone and foundation were blessed by Bishop Nikolai Velimirović, who would become a beloved Saint of the Serbian people.

You would think I would be grateful to God and be more faithful to the church, but like the Hebrews of the Old Testament, I would soon forget His blessing. Instead, I was in church only sporadically and my growing interest in New Age things was creeping into my life. I was working at an art gallery in an area of Philadelphia called Chestnut Hill, and I was part of a very creative crowd. They were into exploring new things and I willingly followed.

Not having the Church as my compass, I was charting into dangerous waters. I decided to consult a psychic and "get a reading" over the phone to see how many kids Tony and I would have and where we would live. It never entered my mind that there was anything wrong with this. Instead of trusting God, I wanted to take things into my own hands and discover the future. I thought that some people were just gifted with clairvoyance. Another reading sticks out in my mind because the woman told me that I was very intuitive and I should develop it so I could help people by doing readings. This was the worst thing she could have said because it encouraged me to study clairvoyance and how to develop intuitive abilities and my interest grew considerably!

The reader's advice led me deeper into the realm of New Age, because soon I was enrolled at a (self-professed) world-leading metaphysical school that she recommended. I took several classes there, and I even received several certificates as a reader or energy healer that I could proudly hang on my wall at home! Later, I became certified in Reiki, the art of natural healing by touch.

The school emphasized Socrates quote, "to know yourself," as the path to happiness. You have to "manifest" what you want in your life. Knowing God wasn't so important. Knowing *yourself* was, so to know yourself, they taught you how to release your negative energy. You have blockages and you have to learn to how to let go of them. To do this, you had to be familiar with your energy centers or chakras, and you had to face your past lives for deep karmic healing. There were classes for everything, including color and sound healing and soul travel. You get the picture — a real cornucopia. But no matter what your interests were, the purpose behind it all was self-improvement. And if you could help yourself, then you could help others. And who doesn't want to do good and help others?

The teachers shared stories of psychic phenomena to hook the students even more. The husband of one teacher could bend spoons with his mind. Another numerology lady could levitate spontaneously. We craved hearing more because it was evidence of the spirit world!

While I was at the school, I shared a dorm room with five other women, and I began to have my own intuitions that something wasn't right. One night I saw a darkish haze in the room hovering and moving over the other women. Thank God it stayed away from me! The next morning, they were all abuzz wondering what the dark cloud could have been and what it meant. I thought it was really strange. Was I the only one who felt scared?

Perhaps my biggest regret about getting involved with this place was convincing one of my gallery girlfriends from Philadelphia to come down and check it out. She came for a week of classes and a reader told her that she and her husband were going to divorce. It became a self-fulfilling prophecy because after she went home, she had an affair which led to the divorce. I always wondered if I was responsible by inviting her. If she had never had that reading, would things have turned out differently for her?

Once you get involved with New Age pursuits, there's no end to it — ever. You just want more and more of the same mistake or sin. In John 8:34 (KJV), Jesus said, "Whosoever committeth sin is the servant of sin," and I definitely became a slave to my New Age masters.

Readers give you advice that takes you deeper into the New Age quicksand. It is subtle, but they tell you things like — wear Amethyst and you will feel less stressed. Buy angel divination cards to help you develop your intuition. Change your home through Feng Shui and you can create new possibilities. Or use creative visualization to enhance your life! You can make anything happen by visualizing and meditating. All these so-called psychics convinced me that I could do the same thing, so I became fascinated. These were abilities that I didn't even know I had! After all, who doesn't want to know what's going to happen if you could? It's so tempting.

I thought these intuitive abilities were gifts from God. I thought everyone had a sixth sense if they could only tap into it. The readings drew me in the most. In the beginning, I felt like I was just satisfying a curiosity, but as my addiction progressed, I couldn't let three months pass without needing another reading. It was gradual through the years. I would tell Mommy and Tony what the reader was saying and they would smile to hide their confusion. But no one blinked an eye, and I continued readings up until my early forties when I finally began to stop. In all, my experiments into psychic abilities lasted over twenty years of my life. It wasn't until our move to Tennessee that God began to speak to me to leave these practices behind for good. Now, as a practicing Orthodox Christian, I feel shame for the years wasted on these things. I know God has forgiven me, but it is a bitter pill to open up my life for all to see and admit how obsessed I was.

I caution all of my readers to avoid any and all New Age pursuits — past life recall, channeling, reiki, psychometry, astrology, gemstones, and energetic flower remedies and so on. I'm baffled that I didn't see the conflicts with my belief in God back then. Each and every one of these things only pulls you away from God. You stop communing with Him and seeking His answers. My curious nature unknowingly pulled me into this world. My consuming desire "to know" caused me to fall into the same original sin that cost Adam and Eve their place in Paradise with God. My parents were never interested in these things, and this was solely my own pursuit. This became the big sin in my life and I still continually ask God for His forgiveness.

On the other hand, however, there is a form of intuition that is revealed to us by God. Since the Serbs have been immersed in the life of the Church for many centuries, they have developed Christian responses to the presence of evil. They cross themselves or sprinkle holy water at their front door. They light a candle for a deceased relative if they dream about them.

I remember in great detail a dream Mommy had a week before Daddy died. The dream was about her much adored, favorite deceased Aunt (Teta) Rada, or Radmila, her mother's sister. She was a school administrator and her husband, Miloš Dragović, was a senator in Belgrade before World War II.

In Mama's dream, Teta Rada (who died some twenty years prior to this dream) was chauffeured in a black limousine to our home in Burlington, North Carolina. She got out of the car, knocked on the door and instead of saying hi to her niece (my mom), she ignored her and went over to my dad, took him by the hand and walked him out of the house and into the black limo. They took off together, leaving my mother standing bewildered on the front steps of the house in her dream.

Mommy told Daddy about the dream, and he told her to go to church the next morning and light a candle for Teta Rada. Of course, she did. One week later, Daddy died of a massive heart attack in the same bedroom where Mama experienced this dream.

Looking back, I think it was my father's death that led me into New Age practices. I was only eighteen when he passed, and I missed him dearly. There was an emptiness in my life without him, and my soul yearned for him. I wondered where he was on the "other side." Could he still speak to me? Could I find him somehow and keep him in my life in some meaningful way?

In the metaphysical practices, this is possible. Mediumship is a gift of famous psychics who lure people in with promises of contact with loved ones who are dead. That was one of the calling cards that attracted me. How foolish I was — a college graduate — buying into to this stuff!

What you permit into your spiritual life requires discernment. Without the teachings of the Church and the guidance of a priest or spiritual father, one can become lost, as I did. I didn't know the difference between seeking out readers to determine the future and a dream that can comfort you or prepare you for difficult times ahead. One is a search of knowledge in the darkness beyond God's light. The other is a revelation given by God out of His divine Grace.

Some might think I have become judgmental towards my friends who practice New Age beliefs. On the contrary, I only judge myself. I remind myself of what Jesus said, "Judge not, that ye be not judged" (Matthew 7:1 KJV). A friend of mine at St. Petka Serbian Orthodox Church in Nashville, Danica Ninkovic, always says, "There are only two individuals that are allowed to judge you in this world: number one is God, and number two is yourself." I like that.

St. Nikolai Velimirović, the most significant Serbian bishop and Saint since St. Sava, the first bishop of Serbia, said, "As Orthodox Christians we must carefully examine every aspect of our involvement in the world, its activities, holidays and festivals, to be certain whether or not these involvements are compatible with our Holy Orthodox Faith." [3] I wish I had known more about St. Nikolai in my younger days. If I had, I would have pondered his words deeply.

There is no need to further elaborate on all the subjects that I was curious about during this twenty-year period of my life. From intuitive readings of future events to past-life regression, they all have the same theme — they take you away from God as God, our Supreme Deity and Creator, the Triune God who fashioned us and breathed life into us.

He is the judge. His will alone orders and knows the future. Not me or you. It is NOT the universe who created us; God made us according to His image and likeness. We are commanded in the Bible not to seek fortune tellers or seers. We are to seek God only. These intuitive explorations only led me to think that I had some sort of gift or natural ability that I could develop like some untapped gold mine within myself. The spotlight was on me and not God. All of these New Age pursuits lead nowhere — only to confusion. You explore yourself ad nauseam only to discover more unanswered questions. These explorations into self only lead to God's absence in your life. Alternatively, our true goal to a life of meaning is clearly stated in the Bible. "Draw nigh to God, and he will draw nigh to you…" (James 4:8 KJV).

The tradition of the ancient Orthodox Christian Church has given us spiritual labors and a liturgical year of feast days and services that yield fruit for our souls and ultimately our salvation. It's through our repentance, fasting, and unending prayers that we develop a special devotion to and knowledge about our Lord God. In this way, we keep Him active in our lives, so we are never far from His teachings. A life immersed in the Church helps us navigate our lives correctly. When all of our senses are focused on Christ, we are continually reminded to pursue him, even in our weakest moments. If it's God's will, He may send us a sign or dream to comfort us. However, we should not seek out these types of things. This is how we negate God's will. We must continually struggle to encounter Him so He is able to abide in us each and every day. Our one and only aim in life should be to achieve salvation.

After I re-ordered my life around Christ and His Church, one of my New Age friends commented, "Ariane, I respect the path you are on now." If I had been courageous then, I would have told her that I am not on *a path*. I am on *the only path* there ever was or will ever be and it is in the name of the Father, the Son and the Holy Spirit. There are no other paths. There is only one Truth. We are not in charge. God is.

Discernment brings change. Once you wake up to the majesty that God is all there is, you understand the need to feed your faith. This is why the Liturgy exists. Our faith is a living thing. We can't just show up once or twice a year to Church and expect to draw near to God or understand the Bible. We must cultivate our faith like a garden. We must strive towards our salvation.

My two children's baptisms were by far the greatest sacramental events in my life after my marriage. As time went on, I noticed the more I read about God or His Saints and participated in the Liturgy, my life became more stable and peaceful. My desire to know the future became almost non-existent as I was completely happy in the present moment.

But it took one significant event for me to completely weed my garden of anything remotely related to intuition, or any of my New Age interests. This was when God spoke to me through my art. I'm an artist and God knew exactly how to reach me. He created a series of events in my life that would lead me to completely awaken to Christ's presence through one of his Saints.

CHAPTER

IV

GOD CAUGHT ME IN HIS THREADS

*"And Jesus, when he was baptized, went up straightway out of the water:
and, lo, the heavens were opened unto him, and he saw the Spirit of God
descending like a dove, and lighting upon him: And lo a voice from heaven,
saying, This is my beloved Son, in whom I am well pleased."*

Matthew 3:16-17 (KJV)

By the time our family moved to Tennessee in 2003, change and spiritual growth were already underway. Initially, I found an Orthodox Church near our new home, but I didn't feel a strong connection to it. A chance encounter led us to our present church, St. Ignatius, in the beautiful countryside near Franklin. My husband Tony, who is a physician, and I went to a fundraising event near his hospital. There were hundreds of people in attendance and eventually we made our way through the crowd to the buffet line. Once through the line, we scanned the room for a place to sit and eat. Not knowing anyone in the sea of faces made me feel anxious. As Tony followed me into the crowd, I softly prayed, "Lord show me where to sit!" Finally, we found a table in the cavernous garage of the home that was hosting the event. Of all places, this is where I first heard of my new church home.

We ended up sitting directly across from two of Tony's colleagues from work. One man's wife kept staring at me, and I wondered if there was something wrong with my blouse. I discreetly made sure all of the buttons were in place, but before I could look up again the woman asked, "Is that an Orthodox cross you are wearing?" "Yes," I said, "and how is it that you recognize an Orthodox cross?" "Because I am Orthodox," she exclaimed.

I began to go to the church that she recommended and I delighted in the fact I could finally understand the Divine Liturgy in English! The more I went, the more I learned, and I thirsted for even more knowledge about God and his Saints. I finally understood the Orthodox Christian rituals my parents had introduced me to as a child. I was so touched with the beauty of our services in English. I loved this same liturgy in Old Slavonic, but I never knew the language well enough to understand the meaning of the service. Now I did, and it pierced my soul and raised my heart and my mind to levels of understanding that I never dreamed possible.

I became less interested in the future and "psychic" intuition. New Age pursuits were no longer my focus. My journey of self-discovery took a backseat, and it slowly began to fade. I became more focused on the pursuit of God. I became interested in great men and women who were dedicated to God. In fact, I began reading about them. I had never read a book about a Saint before. I believe God was laying the groundwork for me to awaken to His living presence. I also began attending church every Sunday when we were home, and I became active in the life of the church. This was a dramatic change for me.

I could not have planned what happened next. Our fourteen-year-old dog was dying of cancer. I loved him so much that I decided to have photos made of him by a professional pet photographer. I found a wonderful woman whose warmth and kindness really connected with me. Somewhere in the conversation, she told me that she went to a famous psychic once a year for a reading. I honestly don't remember how we got on this subject, but in my weakness I asked how much the reader charged. She replied, "$400.00 for thirty minutes." But she added it was well worth it because everything the psychic said came true!

Well, I remember having a sinking feeling in my tummy because I knew I should leave this alone. At this point, I still didn't have a solid grounding in what scripture says about psychics. So, I started wondering how this photographer could afford such ridiculous fees for a reading, and my curious nature took over again. I found the psychic's website and discovered that she channeled a Catholic Saint (although I believe the psychic was Baptist) and I became obsessed with the idea of painting this Saint for her in exchange for a psychic reading. I contacted her, and she agreed!

I was excited with this arrangement to get a reading with such a prominent psychic, but I decided it would also be my last one. Church had reawakened something in me, and now there was another voice speaking to me. Why am I doing this? My mind was torn about it because I felt the pull of Christ and all things Orthodox, yet, I wasn't strong enough to resist the temptation of peeking into the future again.

The Lord said, "He that is not with me is against me; and he that gathereth not with me scattereth abroad" (Matthew 12:30 KJV). It's clear that God wants us to pursue Him only. Otherwise, we are scattered and lost. I knew this in my heart, but I wasn't quite ready to commit my will to His commandments.

When I got the reading, it was a real doozy. She did a past life regression with me and discovered that I was my childhood hero, Russian ballerina Anna Pavlova! And in a previous life, I was a famous iconographer in Constantinople. I even painted the famous Vladimir icon of the Mother of God! The reader got to know me just well enough to try to hook me with these stunning revelations. The devil was so cunning to tempt me with the thought that I could actually be the reincarnation of people I so admired!

But as we agreed, I painted the Catholic Saint, Thérèse of Lisieux. I enjoyed creating her portrait; she was such a delight to learn about as I painted. I felt connected to her. The portrait was completed in record time, but when I shipped it to the psychic, I suddenly was overcome with a sense of personal loss. Suddenly, I missed the experience of painting her. She had become like a lovely friend to me.

To fill the void in my heart, I decided to paint an Orthodox Christian Saint. I wanted to paint a Saint I could relate to in my own faith and heritage. Then I could capture that feeling and hang on to it forever. Well, I was stumped! I could not think of even one Saint I wanted to paint. I sat in my living room and leafed through a Russian book on our cocktail table, hoping to find a Saint there since Russians are predominantly Orthodox Christians. In just a few moments, I saw the beautiful face of Ella Feodorovna, Grand Duchess (1864-1918). She was a contemporary of

Anna Pavlova. In fact, they may have even known each other quite well since they moved in similar social circles. I was quickly intrigued with the Grand Duchess Elizabeth. As I continued to read, I discovered that she was later known as St. Elizabeth, the New Martyr. In that instant, I decided I would paint a large portrait of her.

In contrast to my research about St. Thérèse, I didn't jump in and read everything I could find about St. Elizabeth. Her portrait was for me. What's the rush? I could read about her later. She looked lovely, so I set about studying her features and looking at pictures of her instead of reading about her. I found pictures of her as a child, and I saw her as a young lady with her family. Ella was a German princess and the granddaughter of Queen Victoria of England.

In one photo, I saw how she looked after losing her mother. I saw her sadness. I saw how she looked as a newly engaged woman and then a wife to Sergei, the Grand Duke of Russia. I saw such love between them. I also saw the tragedy in her eyes after he was murdered in 1905 by a socialist revolutionary. Then I viewed a transformed face, when as a widow, she became a nun and began to do the work of Christ. I saw the light around her. I saw radiance and beauty. So I sketched her out. Then I transferred the sketch to a large canvas. Then one grey winter day I began to paint St. Elizabeth.

At first, I didn't see the pure white dove that suddenly appeared to watch me paint. I was aware of a bird staring into our home through the second-floor level transom window where my studio is located; but I thought it was a pigeon, so I gave it no notice. Then Tony, our eight-year-old son said, "Mama there is a white dove — right there," as he pointed to the window. There was a white dove indeed, and I thought *how unusual* since you don't see them outside like a wild bird. And the dove kept coming on the third, fourth and fifth day…the bird would appear in the morning and leave in the early evening only to return the next day. I was intrigued. Maybe I should add him to the painting. So I did. I wanted to know more. All I knew was the bird kept coming as I kept painting.

One evening I finished my work, and I saw the dove. I grabbed my little disposable camera and snapped a shot or two. That night, I logged onto the internet and researched the symbolism of a white dove. I couldn't shake the feeling that God was sending me an important message. The dove is a symbol for peace and the Spirit of God, but I learned that the birds are also used in many types of ceremonies. In Russia, they release white doves after someone dies, for example. I lost track of time and it was getting really late. My husband said, "Come to bed Ariane!" I replied, "I'm just reading about the white dove and wondering what it could possibly mean?" Tony then yelled, "I will tell you! It's obvious! It means the Holy Spirit! Now come to bed!" His small outburst made me smile. Of course, it means the Holy Spirit. That's all I needed to know. Sometimes the obvious is the hardest thing to grasp.

The next morning, after my late-night computer search, the bird was back in the same spot, as usual. I looked at the pure white dove in a new way this time. I could see the Holy Spirit. It was my "eureka" moment! God had sent the Holy Spirit to me as a gift! In my simple mind, I still couldn't really imagine what this meant for me. But I realized the one thing I had to do. I had to stay in the life of the Church and learn all I could about the life of St. Elizabeth the New Martyr. She would be my new mentor. It opened the door to hundreds of Saints as witnesses to Christ whose virtues mentor all of us struggling to live the Christian life. God had hooked and caught me. I was no longer scattered.

I finished the painting of St. Elizabeth by adding a white dove and church in the upper left corner of the painting. I varnished it late one night as the last step. It was done. The next morning, I arose early to walk my dog and in my front lawn, there were white dove feathers strewn across the grass. I would not see the white dove again. I ran into the house and got a small bag and collected a few of the pure white feathers as a remembrance. I came in and sat down, tears streaming down my face. God knew I finished the painting. The white dove's mission was also finished; the message was sent and received by me.

It was so much to digest, and I really didn't know where to begin other than to read about St. Elizabeth the New Martyr. I read every book I could find about her.[1] She was easy to relate to since there are many photographs of her. I would stare into her eyes and see such beauty and such sorrow at the same time. Her eyes spoke volumes to me through time and space. She was a Grand Duchess with great wealth and beauty, but her life was radically altered when her husband, Grand Duke Sergei Alexandrovich, a member of Russian royal family, was assassinated by a bomb that ripped through his carriage. She forgave her husband's murderer and left him an icon of Jesus Christ for his jail cell. Her goodness was hard to grasp. In every area of her life, she followed exactly all of the Lord's commandments. She forgave as he forgave.

I was intrigued with how she handled sorrow. She endured a difficult and beautiful life with a joyful sorrow. She never lost hope. She addressed letters to everyone as, "Dearly beloved in the Lord." That really struck me.

She also responded to her loss by saying *yes* to God. Within four years of Sergei's death, she sold all of her magnificent worldly possessions and used the money to open a convent at which she would serve as abbess. Soon, there was a chapel, hospital, and orphanage at Saints Martha and Mary Convent. For the next nine years, St. Elizabeth ministered to the poor and the most wretched in Moscow. In 1918, the Bolsheviks came for her, and she did not resist. She had opportunities to leave Russia, and she could have escaped, just like our Lord Jesus Christ could have evaded his captors. They threw her and other royal family members into an abandoned mineshaft and she struck a beam on the way down. Lenin's security forces (Cheka) threw grenades into the pit, but from below they heard singing of the Cherubic hymn:

"We, who mystically represent the Cherubim,
And chant the thrice-holy hymn to the Life-giving Trinity,
Let us set aside the cares of life…
That we may receive the King of all,
Who comes invisibly escorted by the Divine Hosts."[2]

If I was about to die, would I be singing? I would probably be screaming and trying to get help. She was so at peace with death. She knew God was in charge. She knew that her body was temporary and her soul immortal, and she lived with the heavenly kingdom ever present in her mind. Her earthly life came to an end in the bottom of that mineshaft. Vassili Ryabov, one of the killers, threw another grenade into the pit after they heard the singing and they built a fire over the opening for good measure to finish off their victims. Her last minutes were spent bandaging the wounds of Prince Ioann Konstantinovich with her own clothing. Later her corpse was pulled out of the hole for a photo opportunity. Her three fingers were frozen in death forming the Holy Trinity, making the sign of the cross.

St. Elizabeth entered heaven with a martyr's crown. She was canonized as a Saint in 1992 by the Moscow Patriarchate, a year after the fall of the Soviet Union (the Russian Church Outside of Russia canonized her in 1981). Her remains are enshrined at the Church of Maria Magdalene on the Mount of Olives in Jerusalem, a church that she and her husband helped build. She is one of ten twentieth-century martyrs honored with a statue at Westminster Abbey.

Because they embody the attributes of Christ, the Saints are given to us by God to show us how to live in Christ and for Christ. The Lord picked St. Elizabeth for me because I already adored and knew everything about Russia, especially the time period in which she lived. The more I learned about her, the more I admired her unbelievable, awe-inspiring love and sincere, pure devotion to God. She became a spiritual mentor to me — a female Christian role model.

As I immersed myself into the life of St. Elizabeth, other God-loving people came into my life. I became acquainted with the Very Reverend Archimandrite Nektarios Serfes, a Greek Orthodox monk, who kindly provided me with reading resources about St. Elizabeth. Father Nektarios, an accomplished writer himself, is also very involved in supporting the Serbian Orthodox Church and the people of Kosovo as President of the Decani Monastery Relief Fund.[3]

He was so moved by my painting of St. Elizabeth, my devotion to her, and the miraculous appearance of the white dove, that he offered me a relic[4] of the Saint as a gift. I was surprised, excited, and speechless! I quickly asked the permission of my parish priest, Father Stephen Rogers, if I could even have a relic in my home. He agreed it was possible. When it arrived, Tony and I opened the package carefully and reverently as we prayed, and a sweet fragrance emanated from it. I commissioned an icon of St. Elizabeth with a space for the relic to be placed inside her cross. My dearest girlfriend and iconographer, Jennie Atty Gelles, who is the sister of the late ArchPriest Alexander Atty, painted the beautiful icon. Jennie studied with the late Ksenia Pokrovsky[5], who was a world-renown Russian iconographer. She was featured in the book *Hidden and Triumphant*[6] as one of the few courageous iconographers who kept the Orthodox Christian faith alive in the Soviet Union by painting the Holy images of God secretly, even under the constant threat of arrest.

After Jennie finished the icon, it needed to be blessed before it was hung in our home. We decided to take it to Saints Joseph and Andrew Carpatho-Russian Orthodox Church in Candler, North Carolina, where Father John Zboyovski could perform this important Orthodox tradition. After he blessed the icon, the relic of St. Elizabeth was placed is a cross-shaped reliquary embedded in the icon.

Upon returning home, I found a statue of a white dove placed by my garden mailbox. Where did this come from? I hadn't told anyone locally the story about the white dove. A lovely neighbor left it there for me as a gift. When I asked her about it, she said, "Oh it was a random selection...I just got it for you because I liked it." We often swap gifts with our neighbors, but this was a special surprise considering everything I had been through with the painting, the dove, the relic, and now the icon. I truly believe God gave me these special spiritual gifts and especially the gift of a white dove — of all things! I believe God blessed me through my kind neighbor as He saw me drawing nearer to Him.

There are no accidents in anything we experience and do. God knows our hearts. There could be other worldly explanations for my experience, but what are the odds of a Tennessee homemaker and artist having a fragment of the body of the granddaughter of Queen Victoria, Sovereign of the United Kingdom and Empress of India, and sister to Empress Alexandra Feodorovna, wife of Nicholas, the last Tsar of Russia? Statistically, the possibilities are infinitely small! How could this happen? God saw me alone in the studio painting every day, awakening to Him with St. Elizabeth leading me along. With God all things are possible, indeed! (Matthew 19:26)

As I continued to grow in the faith, our priest Father Stephen came and blessed our home. Later, he told me he noticed my rather large collection of New Age books that day, and he immediately started praying for me. Not long after the house blessing, I had a vivid dream that startled me. As I fell into a deep sleep one night, I saw floating before my eyes in radiant color and standing in front of me the Most Holy Theotokos and Ever Virgin Mary. There was no question in my mind it was her. Facing me, she showed me a deck of tarot cards. As our eyes locked she said, "Get rid of all of these."

It scared me awake. Every living person and nation should hold the Most Holy Mother of God in the highest regard and love. In Luke 1:48, KJV, Mary says that "all generations shall call me blessed." How could it be that she spoke to me in a dream? Then I wondered, do I have a tarot card deck? Suddenly, I remembered I did. Someone from the art gallery gave me a deck as a going away present when we left Philadelphia. I used to play with them frequently to guess the future for myself.

I ran up to my studio and took the tarot deck and every New Age book and threw them in the large trash can in my garage. I threw away anything that took me away from trusting or turning to God. Everything related to astrology, reincarnation, divination, angel cards, mediums, Feng Shui, and even readings I had on tape — they were all gone and in the trash. It was the end of anything New Age in my life.

At first, I felt ashamed that the Mother of our Lord reprimanded me. I must be a lost cause. I felt sad. However, with time I realized maybe she felt I was worth saving, because I was trying. I just had to finish the job. In church you hear, "Holy things are for the Holy." This applies to your home as well. You glorify God with what you say, what you do, and what is in your home. God must be there. You cannot have unholy things there if you are striving to lead a holy life. So, I was gently corrected with love.

SCRAPBOOK MEMORIES

II

THE SERBIAN-AMERICANS...

Ariane Michelle Trifunovic.

St. Sava, First Archbishop and Enlightener of Serbia. His motto: "Only Unity Saves the Serbs."

Background illustration by Ariane's talented grandfather Lieutenant Colonel Velibor Dobrić of King Peter II (top left) of Yugoslavia and General Draža Mihailović (top right).

Ariane's father, Aleksandar Trifunović, as a young man.

Ariane's dad and maternal grandfather, the 'Colonel,' 1965.

Ariane's paternal grandfather, Ljubomir Trifunović.

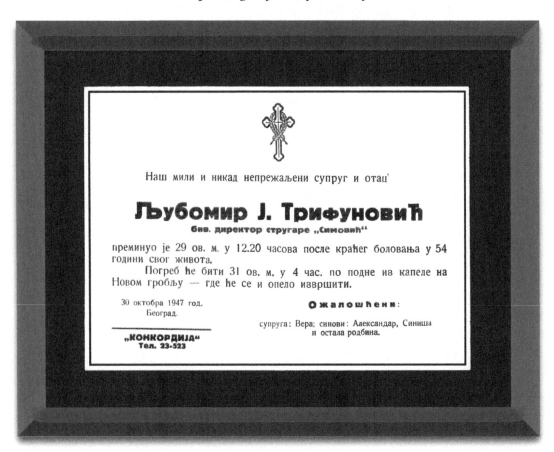

Наш мили и никад непрежаљени супруг и отац

Љубомир Ј. Трифуновић

бив. директор стругаре „Симовић"

преминуо је 29 ов. м. у 12.20 часова после краћег боловања у 54 години свог живота.

Погреб ће бити 31 ов. м. у 4 час. по подне из капеле на Новом гробљу — где ће се и опело извршити.

30 октобра 1947 год.
Београд.

Ожалошћени:

супруга: Вера; синови: Александар, Синиша и остала родбина.

„КОНКОРДИЈА"
Тел. 23-523

Death certificate of Ljubomir Trifunović, printed in Cyrillic.

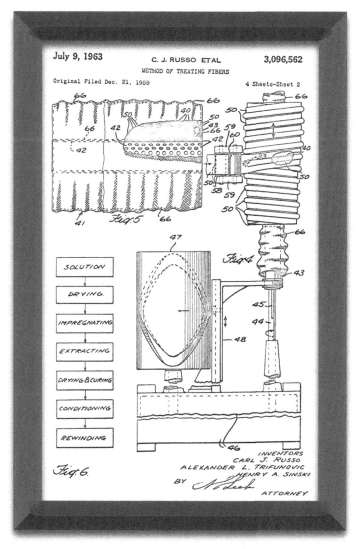

Aleksandar Trifunovic's patent drawing of a textile invention.

Ariane's father at work — at home and abroad — with textile machine technology.

Ban-Lon was Aleksandar Trifunovic's most famous textile invention.

*Ariane's family visits her father's grave at Calumet Park Cemetery in Merrillville, Indiana.
It was her mother's turn to be a widow, pictured here in all black, just like her Aunt/Teta Rada.
Pictured here are (left to right) Ariane's maternal grandmother Darinka, brother Robert,
mother Danica, Ariane, and young cousin Doris, 1982.*

*Teta Rada, Ariane's great aunt, strolling in Beograd/Belgrade with her mother Danica Dobrić.
She wore traditional black widow garments every day after her Serbian Senator husband
was murdered by the communists in 1941.*

Danica Dobrić living in Paris.

Ariane's mother arriving in the U.S. from Paris, 1958.

Danica and her Westie dog, Kraljević Marko (named after the medieval Serbian prince).

Danica Dobric Trifunovic was such an elegant, poised woman.

Ariane's mom all dressed up and ready to celebrate the graduation of both her children in style.

When asked to bring food to a party Ariane's stylish mom either made Serbian cheese pita (pictured) or her famous Russian salad.

Danica was a fashion consultant and shared styling tips with her customers.

The part of the Orthodox Christian marriage where Ariane's parents were "crowned."

Danica and Aleksandar celebrating Christmas early in their marriage.

Ariane's parents having fun in the backyard of their home in Delaware.

Ariane's maternal grandparents celebrating their Slava, St. George.

Young Ariane with her mother Danica (left) and father Aleksandar (right)
and her brother Robert in Delaware.

Ariane holding Jamie (their West Highland White Terrier family dog)
pictured with her brother and maternal grandparents.

A Serbian-American family portrait. Ariane is in center first row.

Ariane with her beloved Deka, the only grandfather she ever knew.

Ariane's maternal grandparents and uncle arrive from Indiana to watch her perform in the "Nutcracker" at the Wilmington Playhouse in Delaware.

A family visit with maternal grandmother and uncle in Merrillville, Indiana — a few years after the death of Ariane's grandfather.

A Trifunovic family portrait in North Carolina.

The last Trifunovic family road trip to their ocean-front South Carolina condo —
shortly afterwards, Aleksandar passed away.

74

Ariane's freshman year portrait, Meredith College, Raleigh, North Carolina.

Ariane with her mother Danica, 1981.

Anna Pavlova. Russian ballerina and Ariane's lifelong inspiration. 1881-1931.

Ariane practicing ballet in her bedroom in North Carolina.

Years of practice helped Ariane achieve dancing goals.

Ariane's uncle, Mike Dobrich, with his handpainted Kosovo art sign.

CHAPTER

V

FROM THE THREADS OF THE OLD WORLD, COME THE NEW

"And he that sat upon the throne said, Behold, I make all things new. And he said unto me, Write: for these words are true and faithful."

Revelation 21:5 (KJV)

Years have gone by now and my children are growing so much! I have tried so far, to the best of my ability, to put God first in all things in our household and show them a life in the Church that encompasses all things. I have taught them the history of the Church and how it has been preserved for them. They know the Nicene Creed, the Church's earliest confession of faith.

The Orthodox Church professes the original Nicene Creed as written by the First and Second Ecumenical Councils. The first was called together in 325 AD by the Roman Emperor Constantine. The emperor was a turning point in Christian history; under him, Christians were given their freedom to worship openly. Before that, from the time of the apostles, the faith had suffered greatly from periodic persecutions by both Jews and Romans. When Constantine came to power, "The Way," which started as a Jewish sect, was becoming the majority religion among the Gentile population of the Roman Empire.

The emperor recognized this and summoned all the bishops of the Church to Nicaea to hammer out their differences. *One empire, one church*, was Constantine's purpose. Their first order of business was to deal with the divinity of Christ. There was a great debate across the empire stirred by Bishop Arius of Alexandria, who taught that Jesus was a separate being created by God. St. Athanasius and the majority of bishops won the day, however, with the Orthodox point of view that Jesus was God incarnate or God in the flesh. The two are of "one essence" as it reads in the Creed. We still say those words today.

Many contemporary Christians don't know the Creed. In fact, many Protestants and non-denominational believers, unknowingly subscribe to a subtle form of the ancient heresy of Arianism. Ask them who Jesus is. Virtually all will reply "the Son of God." That's true, but press on. But *is* he God? Then the waffling begins. They are not entirely comfortable saying it even though Jesus stated clearly that he and the Father are one (John 10:30). We believe in a Triune God — Father, Son, and Holy Spirit. Three persons, but all fully God.

Orthodoxy is Christianity unchanged from its beginning. Jesus is God in the flesh. And because he is God incarnate, born of a virgin, Mary, his mother, is known by her Greek title Theotokos (Bogorodica in Serbian), the God bearer. This central truth and mystery is heard in our worship, the Divine Liturgy, and seen in our iconography. Icons of the Theotokos and Jesus Christ flank the doors to the altar in every Orthodox Church. The Greek letters, O ΩN (or ὁ ὤν), in Jesus' halo, are shorthand for the "One Who Is, without beginning and without end," the Greek translation of God's name spoken to Moses from the burning bush (Exodus 3:14), thus indicating Christ's divinity. The Royal Doors to the altar feature the icon of the Annunciation, because the incarnation made our salvation possible. And above the altar in the apse is the Platytera icon, which symbolizes the infinite Creator God being contained within Mary, making her the "holy of holies" in the flesh. "And the Word was made flesh, and dwelt among us..." (John 1:14 KJV).

It's important to learn our rich history. So many Christians only know their faith from the Bible. In church, they read a text and then zip forward 2,000 years to today without knowing the Church Fathers and Saints who gave their lives during the centuries in between so that we could have a Bible to read or a church to attend.[1]

I make sure that my children see the bigger picture. The church thrived and grew exponentially in the first four centuries without an "official book." Traditions passed down from the time of the apostles through the bishops were the foundation of Christian worship and sacraments. St. Paul said, "Therefore, brethren, stand fast, and hold the traditions which ye have been taught, whether by word, or our epistle" (2 Thessalonians 2:15 KJV). The New Testament came much later in the fifth century when the Church Fathers canonized the four Gospels and letters shared from the beginning by the apostolic churches in order to combat false teachings and novel gospels.

So the Church is the author of the New Testament, and Holy Tradition made it possible. The two go hand in hand. You cannot separate them.

My son and daughter know that their faith is the oldest in Christendom. The Orthodox Church can be traced back to Christ and his disciples. The basic tenets have not changed and the Orthodox Church is the only church that can truly claim this — **nothing subtracted or added. We are the living body of Christ.**

It's a history that can be seen, too. Starting with the time of the Emperor Constantine, the Church became the faith of the Byzantine Empire. The oldest churches and monasteries still standing in Jerusalem, Mt. Sinai, Istanbul (Constantinople), and Greece, the Christian East, are testaments to Christianity's Orthodox roots. Their architecture and iconography are consistent with Orthodox worship today.

There are millions of books and letters written by patriarchs, bishops, priests, and monks documenting Christian history. You can read and understand how the Saints preserved the faith from generation to generation. There was only one church for over 1,000 years until there was a division between Rome (Catholic) and Constantinople (Orthodox) in 1054. Byzantium collapsed for good in 1453 when Ottoman invaders sacked the capital, Constantinople, but the Orthodox Church persevered.

In Christianity's second millennium, Orthodoxy spread to Russia, the Far East, and finally to America. The first Orthodox missionaries in North America were Russian monks and priests that came to Alaska. The continental United States welcomed the Church with waves of immigrants from Greece, Russia, Serbia, Romania, Bulgaria, and other countries. Churches were the center of their communities. Orthodox parishes today still hold to their traditions and culture, but they are blended churches with growing numbers of converts. The Antiochian Church in America, including the church I attend, is virtually all English-speaking converts.

I want my children to feel at home in any Orthodox Church. The Divine Liturgy is the same in every church, no matter the language, whether English, Greek, or Serbian. There are minor differences based on local traditions, but the worship and theology are the same. There are no "denominations" in Orthodoxy.

The Orthodox faith is a God-centered faith structuring life around the Church. Everyone plans according to the secular calendar of seasons and holidays, such as the fourth of July, Labor Day, and Thanksgiving, but Orthodox Christians know the time of the year based on the liturgical calendar of feast days and fasts as well. Pascha (Easter), the celebration of our Lord's resurrection, is preceded by Lent, forty days of fasting, and Holy Week, seven days of strict fasting and long services following the Passion of Christ. Pentecost and Ascension are next. Then there's the shorter Apostles' Fast. August is marked by the Lord's Transfiguration and another short fast leading up to the Dormition of the Theotokos. And then we look forward to another forty-day fast and Christ's Nativity or Christmas. In between, every day is a commemoration of a Saint or an important event in the life of the Church. Most Wednesdays and Fridays are also strict fast days in memory of Jesus' betrayal and crucifixion.

Opportunities for prayer and worship abound. In addition to the Divine Liturgy every Sunday, liturgies are celebrated on all the major feast days. Many evenings will include Vespers or some other form of prayer service. Through all of these beautiful services, we go through the Bible repeatedly in chanting and readings. If you think your church is a "Bible church," attend an Orthodox church for a season and compare how much scripture is heard! A life in the liturgical year, in the feast days of the Church, is a life in the Bible.

If one lives according to the Church calendar, God truly permeates your soul. Prayers and daily scripture are read in front of the icons we have in our homes. Altogether, the services, sacraments, prayers, and readings act as a compass to keep us on course. Otherwise, we can become lost, like a hiker without a map. We are made in God's image and by abiding in Him, we become more like Him. But we need direction and the Church provides that.

We also need the Church to interpret the Bible for us. The setting must be the Liturgy. The Word can only be understood in the context of the Church. "Sola Scriptura," the foundation of the Protestant movement, says that the Bible alone is sufficient for Christian doctrine. People can read scripture and the Holy Spirit will tell them what it means. That sounds good, but ask ten people to read a difficult passage and you're likely to get ten interpretations! Can the Holy Spirit reveal multiple truths?

It's interesting to note that the Reformation (starting in 1517 AD) caught fire not long after the beginning of the information revolution. Guttenberg's printing press was invented around 1450-55 AD. The ability to read and privately own books and pamphlets liberated the minds of the masses, but it weakened many Western institutions, particularly the Catholic Church. Before this time, the Bible, which was copied by hand, was only read or heard in church as the central authority of information. The Reformation meant freedom from papal control.

The rise of individualism has only accelerated in the age of the internet and social media. Our society is obsessed with individual rights. It's the "me generation." Selfies… look at me! And don't tell me what to do or think, either! The more self-centered people are, the more godless the world becomes.

I'm excited, however, to have an anchor, my faith in God and trust in Christ's Holy Church to help me understand His word. I think about how many times as a young person that I ignorantly didn't put God first and did so many stupid things. I was truly lost. Now I live in the present moment. Salvation is an ongoing process, moment by moment, of walking towards God. It's a life-long pursuit. Being "born again" is just the beginning. You have to work at being a Christian. St. Paul tells us we have to run the race to win.[2] You can't win if you don't finish the race! You must awaken every day to a great love or pull towards God and work to keep His commandments.

After the dove visitation, Mommy observed that I was going to church a lot more and that I was taking the children. Since St. Ignatius is an Antiochian Orthodox parish with mostly English-speaking American converts, she wondered if it was a real Orthodox Church (Pravoslavna Crkva). Since she grew up in Yugoslavia under communist oppression, she remembers all too well how careful Christians had to be when practicing their faith. They couldn't be too "showy" about it. Speaking openly about issues of faith was just unheard of; when she was a young girl, being too religious could land you in a Tito jail. Her grandmother Natalia, who was the wife of a priest, told her than even if the authorities closed all the churches, communion with God was still possible. She could still pray, even in her closet. But times have changed and in a free country, Orthodox Christians can practice their faith openly.

Mama only knew ethnic Orthodoxy — Serbian, Greek, or Russian. She thought Americans weren't Orthodox. I reassured her that an Orthodox Church in Tennessee was the same faith she was raised in, even if the service was in English and perhaps even in a Southern accent! She had no understanding of the explosive growth of Orthodoxy in the United States over the past fifty years. People are searching for the early Christian Church and they are finding it![3]

The growth of Orthodoxy beyond its ethnic roots is a trend with momentum in the West. When Mama would question these things, I found security in scripture. "There is neither Jew nor Greek, there is neither bond nor free, there is neither male nor female: for ye are all one in Christ Jesus." (Galatians 3:28 KJV) We share one nature in Christ, no matter what language or ethnicity. We are all one in Christ. Just as the worship and theology are the same in the ethnic churches, so it is the same in English-speaking parishes. We are all part of the Ancient Christian Church, the Orthodox Faith.

St. Nikolai Velimirović (Sveti Nikolaj in Serbian), who is considered to be the greatest of modern Serbian Orthodox Saints, was born in Serbia in 1881, but he reposed in the U.S. in 1956. As a Serbian bishop, he spoke frequently to large Western audiences. He was so loved by his countrymen, the Nazis arrested him during World War II and held him for a time at Dachau, the infamous concentration camp. Once he regained his freedom, however, he chose to live in the West and not return to the unfolding nightmare of post-war communist Yugoslavia. He was a brilliant representative of Orthodoxy to Western Europeans and Americans during his lifetime.[4] He saw the future of Orthodoxy when he said, "Let us now turn our gaze from the East to the Far West (America)."[5]

In "The Orthodox Church in America and Its Future," St. Nikolai expresses deep gratitude to all Orthodox immigrants who helped build this country and plant the Ancient Faith into the soil of the New World. But even during his time in America, he saw the need for Orthodox churches to adopt English as their primary language for the next generation, the American children and grandchildren born of immigrants.

He even saw a future where the ethnic churches would come together as one great American Church. "The time may not be far off when there will be a united Orthodox Church in America, which will include all the present Eastern national churches in this country, a Church with one central administrative authority. I see a tendency toward such an end in each of our now individual churches. ... And when by God's Providence the time is ripe for the accomplishment of such a unity, I dare not doubt that the venerable heads of all our Orthodox Churches in Europe, Asia, and Africa, always led by the Holy Spirit, will give their blessing for the organization of a new and autonomous sister Church in America."[6]

That still may be difficult today since it would require the merger of church hierarchies and overlapping dioceses. At the parish level, however, I can see a desire for this.

In the past, Orthodox churches were primarily ethnic. The only Anglo members were people who married into the church. But since the 1970s, there has been a seismic shift of converts to Orthodoxy from Catholic and Protestant traditions. As I said earlier, Antiochian churches, like the one I attend, is virtually all English-speaking converts. The Greek church in Nashville, Holy Trinity, is a very blended church now; Greek-Americans are the minority. The priest is a convert as well. The church retains the Greek language as a matter of tradition, but most of its services are in English.

As the changes continue, there could be a day, as St. Nikolai envisions, where ethnic traditions give way to a new American identity.

With an eye on the West as the future of Orthodoxy, St. Nikolai also appealed to American Orthodox youth to keep their hope in the Church.

America is a pluralistic society and our traditional Christian values no longer represent the majority view. On the great moral issues of our time, abortion and gay marriage, conservative Christians have lost in the arena of public opinion. In fact, anyone with a traditional Christian opinion on these matters now faces ridicule and persecution. Our country is quickly becoming amoral. Materialism, sexual freedom, and public atheism are the new norms.

But even as a minority, we have a role to play as witnesses to the truth. Jesus called his followers "salt." As salt preserved food in Biblical times, we preserve society by being models of decency and charity. Jesus also calls us "light." We are beacons in dark times and we must continue to let our lights shine.[7]

God will not hold His judgment forever. Before his return, Jesus said our world will be like the "days of Noah before the flood."[8] In terms of violence and immorality, we are headed quickly in that direction, if we are not already there. So we must cling to the Orthodox Church. It is our ark, our protection against what will come.

St. Nikolai continued, "The greatest struggle of America these days is the struggle for the priority and superiority of spiritual and moral values…in other words, for predominance of the spiritual over the material, of goodness over cleverness. The Serbs often say that a clever man is as *clever as the devil*. They never say that he is *good as the devil*."[9]

"These are the fundamentals upon which you can build your individual and communal happiness. And you have received these fundamentals as a glorious heritage, never to part with. By practicing this spiritual heritage in your daily life, you will become an adornment to America. And through you, all Americans will come to know and appreciate our ancient Church of the East and her spiritual heroes, (the Saints)."[10]

St. Nikolai, as a bridge between East and West, speaks straight to my heart as a Serbian American Orthodox Christian. All of the Saints of the Orthodox Church are models of sanctity that we must strive to follow. They are our purest examples of a life in Christ. It's this glorious ancient Christian heritage of mine that I pray will always be cherished by my children and their children — from generation to generation. Let them become an adornment to America or wherever they will live. Let them always know and appreciate the Ancient Church of the East as the "pearl of great price."[11]

CHAPTER

VI

THE BLESSING OF MY PEOPLE

"Be ye followers of me, even as I also am of Christ."
1 Corinthians 11:1 (KJV)

St. Paul told the Church in Corinth to follow his example if they wanted to be Christ-like. Some might say that was boastful of him to say, but he was speaking about a truth that we still hold dear in the Orthodox Church. The Church offers its Saints as icons of Christ for us to emulate. By immersing ourselves into the lives of the Saints, we become more like them, and thus more like our Savior Jesus.

It is, in fact, how we are "saved." We are all made in the image of God, but our likeness of Him is tainted by sin. By following the examples of His Saints, we acquire the Holy Spirit, and become more like the God-man, Jesus Christ. Many of the early Church Fathers, some as early as the second century, including St. Irenaeus of Lyons, St. Clement of Alexandria, St. Justin Martyr, St. Athanasius of Alexandria, and even St. Augustine, described salvation as "God becoming human, so that we might become like God."[1] This transformation by divine grace is called theosis or deification, and it is essential Orthodox theology. This is the sacred truth the bishops carried with them to the First Ecumenical Council in 325 to champion Christ's divinity against Arianism, the heresy that claimed that Jesus Christ is not the only-begotten Son of God and one of the Trinity, but is instead a creation of God the Father who started existing at some point in time and, therefore, could not possibly be equal with the Father.

From generation to generation, the Church has produced its Saints to show us the way. Metropolitan Kallistos Ware speaks about the "apostolic succession of the spiritual fathers and mothers…stretching from the apostolic age to our own day, which St. Symeon the New Theologian termed the 'golden chain' and…it is through their interaction that the life of the Church on earth is accomplished."[2]

This "golden chain" includes many Saints from my family's homeland. Their contribution to the faith is a rich deposit of Serbian Orthodox spirituality. My re-discovery of them and other Saints has given me spiritual depth and purpose in life. From St. Sava, the founder of the independent Serbian Orthodox Church in the thirteenth century to St. Nikolai Velimirović in the twentieth century, they have helped me understand what it means to be truly Christian…and truly human as God intends us to be.

The history of Serbia and the Serbian Orthodox Church is too extensive for a deep exploration in this book, but St. Sava permeates our culture and religion, so I have to begin with him. Who is St. Sava? Imagine George Washington and Billy Graham rolled up into one person. Because of him Serbia has a national identity, but I wonder how many Serbs really know his story. I meet too many Serbs who are proud of their heritage, and they even have an icon or two in their homes, but they know very little about our faith and how we became an Orthodox Christian nation.

Christianity took root in the Balkans in the ninth century through missionaries Saints Cyril and Methodius, who invented the Cyrillic alphabet and translated the faith into the Slavic language. Christianity blossomed under the jurisdiction of the Byzantine Patriarch of Constantinople to the east. By the time Rastko Nemanjić was born in the late twelfth century, the Serbian Church was Orthodox, but it was largely administered by outsiders, Greeks and Byzantines. Serbia was still not even a kingdom or nation yet, even though a large part of it was ruled by his powerful father, Grand Prince Stefan Nemanja.

Rastko was one of Stefan's three sons, so he was destined to be a wealthy prince and ruler, but he turned his back on riches and power at the age of seventeen to become a monk on Mt. Athos, a community of monasteries in Greece. Rastko took on a new name, Sava, and when his father Stefan gave up power, he joined his son there as a monk. Together, they built a Serbian monastery, Hilandar, on Mt. Athos, which still stands to this day. After Stefan died, St. Sava returned his body to Stundenica Monastery in Serbia. Then known as St. Simeon, the former ruler remained, even in death, a powerful symbol of Serbian unity and a source of many miracles.

Later, God would use St. Sava to create the Serbian kingdom and church. He persuaded Patriarch Manuel I of Constantinople, who moved his throne to Nicaea in the wake of the Fourth Crusade, to grant independence to the Serbian Orthodox Church in 1219 so that Serbs could serve as priests and determine the destiny and leadership of their own Church. St. Sava served as its first Archbishop until his death in 1235.[3]

While at Mt. Athos, St. Sava developed a plan of governance for both church and state. He translated the Nomocanon, a book which contains all the rules or canons for the governance of the church, from Greek into the Slavonic language. Among the Slavs, St. Sava's translation became known as the Zakonopravilo, and it created a blueprint for the Serbian church and nation. It remains in use in the Serbian, Bulgarian, and Russian Orthodox Churches still today. As Archbishop, St. Sava also crowned his brother Stefan as the first King of Serbia in 1220.

Through St. Sava, an Orthodox kingdom was born. His blending of religion and nationalism is known as Svetosavlje.[4] But of all the great things he accomplished, I'm drawn to his humility and thirst for God. Unlike the rich young ruler who couldn't give up his worldly possessions to follow Christ in the Gospels,[5] St. Sava gave up everything to live the ascetic life on Mt. Athos. He wasn't seeking greatness, but because he was willing to become a servant, God exalted him among men as chief diplomat and spiritual leader of his people. He truly is the "Enlightener of Serbia."

The new Serbian kingdom grew in size and power in the next 150 years. At its zenith, it even included most of Greece due to the weakening of the Byzantine Empire by Latin Crusaders from the West and Muslim invaders from the East. The Crusaders would hold Jerusalem and the Holy Land for a time, but the Ottoman tsunami was washing over much of Byzantium into Eastern Europe. By the end of the fourteenth century, Constantinople was a Christian island in an Ottoman sea. The growing Muslim empire also had its sights on Serbia for more conquest and converts.

The Balkan kingdoms were no match for the Ottoman Empire in terms of trained soldiers, weaponry, and sheer numbers. By the time the Muslim horde approached Serbian territory, the kingdom was no more than a loose confederation of regional rulers, so mounting a defense was a challenge in itself. There weren't many fortresses in Serbia either, because its kings had been too busy building churches and monasteries since the time of St. Sava.

After a number of smaller engagements, Serbs first clashed with the Ottomans on the banks of the Maritsa River (border of Greece and Bulgaria) in 1371 and were beaten soundly. The next major battle was on Serbian soil, and one man firmly believed it was better to die free, than to be enslaved by the Muslim invaders. His name was Prince Lazar Hrebeljanović and he rallied sizable troops of Serbs to meet the Ottoman Turks in a decisive battle on the field of Kosovo in 1389. It would have been easier for Lazar to negotiate and capitulate but, according to ancient tradition, an angel appeared and asked him to choose between the earthly kingdom and the heavenly kingdom. Lazar chose eternity, so he led his forces to the Field of Blackbirds to make a stand for Christendom. Before the battle, Tsar Lazar and his troops celebrated Liturgy and took communion for the "Honorable Cross and Golden Freedom." Kosovo, or Vidovdan as Serbs know it, was seen as a spiritual battlefield.

On June 28, the armies met. There were heavy losses on both sides and Sultan Murat I lost his life, but ultimately the Ottomans won. Lazar was captured and beheaded for his defiance.[6] Eventually, all of Serbia fell to Muslim rule, and their civil and religious oppression continued for the next 400 years. Lazar's remains eventually were taken to Ravanica Monastery where as a Saint and martyr, he continued to be a powerful symbol, like St. Sava, for Serbia's yearning for independence and freedom. St. Lazar's relics at Ravanica remain incorrupt to this day.

This history is important to understanding why Kosovo is *so important* to Serbs. It's not just the site of an important battlefield like Gettysburg or the Alamo in America. Field of Blackbirds is a deeply spiritual place for Serbian souls.

It is vital to understand the sacrifice St. Lazar made. He chose to die as a Christian rather than live as a Muslim at the point of a sword. Through him, the Serbian people developed a national identity of martyrdom. They chose to accept self-sacrifice and death, which is not considered defeat, but the emergence of spiritual idealism — a source of new life and a hope in the final triumph of justice and truth, of those values which belong to the Kingdom of Heaven.[7]

Up until 2014, the priest at St. Petka, the Serbian Orthodox parish in Nashville, was a Hieromonk, Father Serafim Baltic from New Gracanica Monastery outside of Chicago. Father Serafim, who is now Hegumen (or Abbot) at the monastery, speaks about the spiritual history of the Serbian nation, and he describes the concept of "martyric ethos" as a characteristic of so many faithful Serbs over the centuries. Father Serafim's description of the mindset of a martyr was inspired by a lecture given by Metropolitan Amfilohije of Montenegro in Chicago.

It's a concept difficult to grasp for Americans because we live in a continental fortress far away from enemies who wish us harm. We are not immune to attack, as 9/11 proved, but no one can imagine our nation being invaded by an overwhelming Muslim army.

Such is not the case for minority Christians in Syria and Iraq today, as the new self-proclaimed caliphate, ISIS, has murdered, executed, and displaced Christians in a systematic purge reminiscent of Muslim conquests of the past. Dying for Christ is a reality again in the Middle East. Christianity, which has been in Syria since the time of the Apostles, is on the verge of extinction there, and the mass exodus of refugees from the region has created an on-going crisis in Europe.

Some American leaders won't say we are at war with radical Islam, but they are at war with us…and everyone else in their path. It is a war with no end as well. Do you realize how close we were to all being Muslim? In 732, Charles "The Hammer" Martel defeated the Umayyad Caliphate at the Battle of Tours in north central France, preserving Christianity in Western Europe. If it weren't for Charles, Islam by conquest would have pierced the heart of Medieval Europe.

Seven hundred years later, the Ottoman Empire tried to do the same from the East. The Turks didn't stop in Serbia. Throughout the time of Serbia's Muslim occupation, the Ottomans fought wars with Hungary, Austria, Poland, and Venice while controlling a large portion of Eastern Europe until the 1800s when the Empire began to decline. One of their legacies, however, is a significant population of Muslim descendants in Albania, Bosnia, and Kosovo, which has led to new conflicts in modern times.

During the Turkish occupation of Serbia, there was never real peace. Christians who refused to convert, if they weren't jailed or executed, were heavily taxed for not bending a knee to the Prophet Mohammed. The Serbs rebelled in 1594 under a flag that bore the image of St. Sava. In an effort to conquer the Serbian spirit once and for all, the Ottomans took the relics of St. Sava from Mileševa Monastery and ordered Orthodox monks to lead a procession to Belgrade; many of the monks were beaten or killed along the way. When they reached Vračar Hill, they built a pyre and burned the holy Saint's relics in a wooden coffin. The smoke could be seen as far away as the Danube River.

The atrocity did not stand. It only endeared St. Sava even more in Serbian hearts. The resistance continued and Serbia eventually won its independence again in the 1800s. The Serbian people survived. The Serbian Orthodox Church of St. Sava survived. Today, on the site where the Turks burned his relics, stands the Church of St. Sava, one of the largest Christian churches in the world.

What does all this mean to me, a Serbian American Orthodox Christian, artist, suburban housewife, and mother? No one is pointing a gun at my head because I'm a Christian. If I am to intimate Christ, the Saints are my examples, and Saints Sava and Lazar offer me deep lessons to apply in my everyday life. St. Sava gave up worldly possessions and position to follow Christ. Am I willing to do the same? Or do I put money, material things, and social acceptance ahead of my faith? St. Lazar gave up his earthly life for the Kingdom of Heaven. Dying as a martyr may not be a reality for me, but am I ready to put God first in my life no matter the consequences?

Father Serafim says that today's Orthodox mindset should be one of a "living martyrdom." Suffering for Christ is our witness to America. We live in a nation where religious liberty is cherished, but our values are coming under attack more and more in an increasingly agnostic and atheistic society. Are you ready to face scorn, prejudice, and legal harassment for being a Christian? Are you strong enough to live a life of purity when the majority around you thinks that immorality is normal and acceptable? You can and you will, if you pray to Saints Sava and Lazar to help you.

Christians have died for following Jesus from the beginning. St. Stephen was stoned by Jewish zealots. The Romans decapitated St. Paul and crucified St. Peter upside down. That may not be our fate. But St. John, the disciple whom Jesus loved, was exiled to the Isle of Patmos, to die alone. Being ostracized, losing a job, living alone are the possible costs to being a Christian in the West today. Christ prophesied that his Church would be persecuted.[8] It has…it is…it will be persecuted until the end of time.

Jesus said we must "take up our cross" to follow him[9] *before* his crucifixion, so I'm sure it was a confusing statement for the people who heard it for the first time. Crucifixion under Roman occupation of Palestine was reserved for criminals and insurrectionists. Why would I have to die a horrible death to follow this charismatic rabbi and healer? In hindsight, we can see what he meant. There can be many crosses for us to bear in our lives — misfortune, loneliness, persecution, and disease to name a few. Suffering is part of the human condition. It is how we endure these sufferings that transform us into the likeness of Christ. "Father, forgive them; for they know not what they do…"[10]

Serbia has suffered greatly as an Orthodox nation. After winning its full independence from the Ottoman Turks in 1867, Serbia enjoyed freedom and peace only for a short time. There were the Balkan Wars of 1912 and 1914, and then the

First World War pitted Serbia against Austria-Hungary, allies of Germany. This led to the Kingdom of Yugoslavia under King Peter I. A few years later in 1934, King Aleksandar I was assassinated by a Bulgarian terrorist while on an official visit to France, and afterwards Yugoslavia was sucked into the misery of World War II. The occupation of Nazi Germany, with its fascist Italian and Croat allies, created even more suffering. And then after the war, Yugoslavia was subjugated to communist oppression behind the Iron Curtain for almost forty years until the death of strongman Josip Broz Tito in 1980 and the break-up of the nation.

It is so tragic to think of how much blood is in the Serbian soil. My own family experienced martyrdom in the turmoil as well. I've mentioned him earlier in the book, but my great-grandfather (on my mother Danica's side), was the Very Reverend Trandafil Kocić, a Serbian Orthodox priest. He's an important person in my life, and I have always kept a picture of him in every home in which I have lived. As a kid, I would stare at my great-grandfather's photo a lot because Mommy often spoke of him. His mysterious, handsome face was thought provoking; he reminded me of Tsar Nicholas II, the last Tsar of Russia, whom I adore. He looked so kind, and I loved how beautiful his hands were. I felt a deep bond with him. There has always been an unspoken connection with him.

Trandafil Kocić was a history teacher at first, but everyone told Deda (Grandfather) Trandafil he should be a priest because he had such a beautiful, melodic voice that commanded attention. After he became a priest, people would ask if he was serving Liturgy because they wanted to be in church to hear his beautiful voice chanting or giving a homily. This was an important story my mother and her brother, my Uncle Mike or Mihailo, preserved for me, since their mother passed it down to them with great love. There were hopes in the family that Uncle Mihailo would follow his path into the priesthood because he has such a beautiful voice as well. Uncle Mike never felt called to be a priest, but he did become a teacher, so maybe Deda Trandafil did pass down to him some important genes.

My great-grandfather's beautiful voice was silenced in 1915, however, when war broke out between Serbia and its neighbor Bulgaria. The two Orthodox kingdoms were rivals at times; for most years, however, the relationship was friendly. St. Sava was actually visiting there when he died in 1235. But periodically there would be conflict, and in 1915, it was particularly savage. Father Trandafil's home of Leskovac was occupied and in an attempt to "Bulgarize" the Serbs, the Bulgarians murdered my great-grandfather and over 150 other Serbian priests, since they were the pillars of their communities. The attack became known as the "Gorge of Surdulica."

The murder — the martyrdom — of my great-grandfather certainly left an impression on our family, but it also left a permanent, physical mark on my grandmother Darinka, who was only ten years old when the slaughter took place.

When the Bulgarians came for her father, her mother Natalia screamed for her to come in from the yard where she was playing. She ran to the house in such a panic that she slammed the back gate on her left pinkie finger, cutting off the top of it. My grandmother Darinka never forgot that day, and we will remember it always as well. The people of Leskovac remember it, too; they named the street my family lived on after my great-grandfather.

My mother still enjoys telling the story. A few years ago, my priest at St. Ignatius in Franklin, the Very Revered Stephen Rogers, visited our new lake house to bless it, and I brought Mommy along. It was the first time she really talked openly with him, and it was a blessing, since it had taken her awhile to get used to the idea that not all Orthodox are ethnic. It was just a foreign concept to her. But because Father Stephen is such a wonderful priest, his quiet manner disarmed her a bit. She cried as she talked about her maternal grandfather. She also said she could not forgive herself and regretted not taking me or my brother to Surdulica in Serbia to see the monument tomb where he was martyred. Even though her grandfather Trandafil is not yet recognized as a Saint by the Orthodox Church, he still died for his faith, just like St. Lazar, and she still wishes she could return to Serbia to venerate (honor) him. Sadly, that time has passed, but it was wonderful to hear her keep his memory alive once more, considering how much she has struggled with dementia in recent years.

I decided to dedicate the book to my great-grandfather and others like him who were murdered just for being Christian priests. He is one of the many unsung Saints that most people know very little about. I believe my great-grandfather, the Very Reverend Trandafil Kocić, is one of the "unknown" Saints. Some Saints God shows us, and others He does not. In any case, those who have sacrificed so much have a special grace from God and, most importantly, they serve as an example to us. They invite and inspire us to live a Christian life.

Some might see it as a mere coincidence, but is interesting to note that the date of my great-grandfather's murder, November 17, is also my wedding date in the Serbian Orthodox Church. I believe that it was no accident my husband and I were married on the day my great-grandfather was martyred for the Kingdom of Heaven. In God, there are no accidents…everything has deep meaning in our lives. God has a timing for all things.

There is more I want to say in the next chapter about the Saints, who are a blessing in my life, and when God opened my eyes to how He has worked through the Serbian people, a suffering people that survived centuries of enslavement under the Ottoman Turks, as well as periodic oppression from its European neighbors. I truly cherish my Serbian Orthodox heritage.

Through all the twists and turns of history, what matters most is that the Serbs preserved their faith in the Lord Jesus Christ. They always remembered God by celebrating Slava with their family and friends. They celebrated in public when they were free; they did it privately when they were under Turkish rule. Ever since their ninth century conversion, they have clung to their Orthodox roots when it would have been so much easier to be Catholic, Muslim, or atheists during the years of occupation and oppression. The Serbs are a sanctified people who put God first. Now *that's* something to be proud of!

For the Serbian people, faith in Jesus Christ has always meant choosing the path of self-sacrifice, according to the examples of Saints Sava and Lazar. By imitating them, they imitate Christ. It is the path to salvation. Jesus said, "…whosoever will lose his life for my sake shall find it" (Matthew 16:25 KJV).

St. Nikolai Velimirović, when remembering Kosovo, said, "Read your history as you should and you will see the entire law of God engraved on it…awaken spiritually, therefore, and do not immerse your soul in the earthly kingdom…elevate yourselves, O royal people, to the heights of the heavenly kingdom, where truth, holiness, and goodness glisten."[11]

In choosing which kingdom to serve, the Saints point us to theosis, the process of salvation. St. Justin Popović, a student of St. Nikolai and one of Serbia's greatest modern theologians, writes, "The lives of the Saints are nothing more than the life according to Christ the Lord repeated in every Saint in greater or lesser degree, in this or that form, or more precisely: it is the life of Christ the Lord continued through the Saints, the life of the incarnate Word of God, the God-man Jesus Christ, Who became a human being so that as a human being He might give and grant us His divine life; so that as God, by His life, he might illumine, deify and sanctify our human life on earth, *for the One Who sanctifies and those who are sanctified share a common origin*" (Hebrews 2:11).[12]

When I awakened spiritually and fully realized the choices Saints Sava and Lazar made, I knew I had the exact same destiny. From now on, I have to choose to place God or the "Kingdom of Heaven" *first over* everything else in my life! I pray that my future generations will make this same choice as well!

SCRAPBOOK MEMORIES

III

A New Generation...

Bishop Nikolai Velimirović (canonized in 2003) blessing the foundation of St. Nicholas Serbian Orthodox Church where Ariane and Tony married.

Ariane's wedding at St. Nicholas Serbian Orthodox Church, Philadelphia, Pennsylvania, 1990.

Ariane and her husband Anthony Montemuro, M.D., an answer to her prayer.

Danica enjoying two of her grandchildren,
Tony and Ana, on her Tennessee home back porch swing.

Three generations — Ana, Ariane, Danica, and Tony's mother Peggy.

Ariane celebrating Slava St. Petka in Philadelphia with her mother, 1991.

Ariane celebrating her Slava St. Petka with Serbian priest Father Aleksandar Vujkovic
of St. Petka Serbian Orthodox Church, Nashville, Tennessee, 2015.

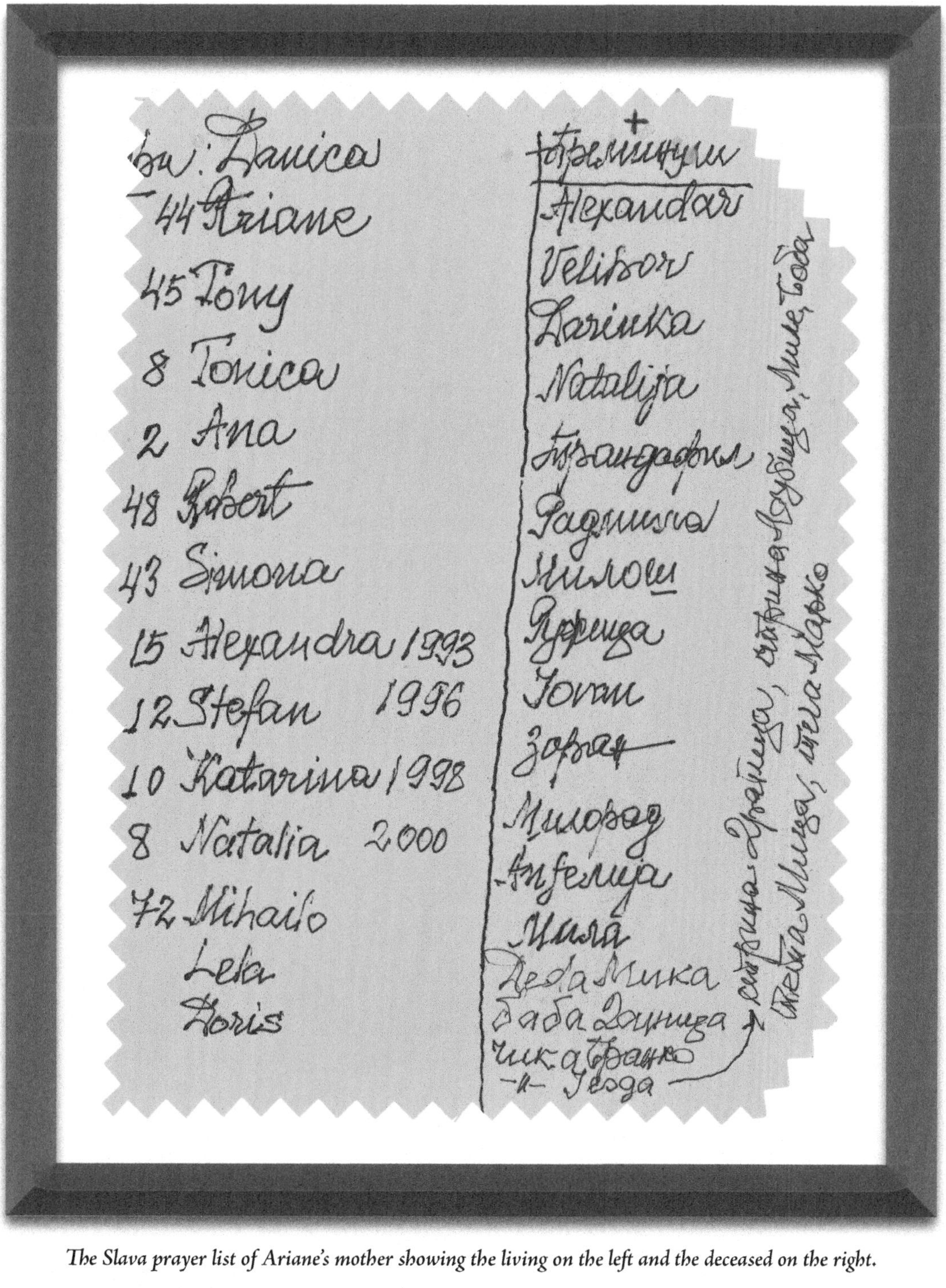

sv: Danica
-44 Ariane

45 Tony

8 Tonica

2 Ana

48 Robert

43 Simona

15 Alexandra 1993

12 Stefan 1996

10 Katarina 1998

8 Natalia 2000

72 Mihailo
Lela
Doris

+
Alexandar
Velibor
Darinka
Natalija
Александра
Радмила
Милош
Радмила
Jован
Зоран
Милорад
Анђелија
Миља
Деда Мика
Баба Даница
Чика Бане
-и- Деда

стрина Драгица, стрина Љубица, Миле, Баба
Тетка Мица, стрина Марко

The Slava prayer list of Ariane's mother showing the living on the left and the deceased on the right.

Ariane's spiritual mentor Grand Duchess Elizabeth of Russia,
future St. Elizabeth the New Martyr.

Photo of the actual dove that visited Ariane's home while she painted St Elizabeth the New Martyr (below). The dove reminded Ariane of the presence of the Holy Spirit in her life.

*Ariane's oil painting of St. Elizabeth the New Martyr —
the first Orthodox Christian Saint she ever painted.*

Ariane with Father Stephen Rogers
of St. Ignatius Antiochian Orthodox Church in Franklin, Tennessee.

Orthodox Christian friends meet in Tennessee.
Ariane with Father Serafim Baltic, Abbot of New Gracanica Monastery,
and co-author Tim Weeks (right).

*Ariane spent a period of time following New Age philosophy.
This influence can be seen in her paintings from that time.*

*During Ariane's New Age period, she transferred several of her paintings to textiles,
such as bags, pillows, wall hangings, and more.*

Father Nektarios Serfes (right) presents one of Ariane's paintings to Abbess Anastasia of Dević Monastery in Kosovo.

"St. Nikolai Velimirović, Apostle from Lelić"
Oil painting by Ariane
A copy of Ariane's painting of St. Nikolai is now at Dević Monastery in Kosovo (see preceding page).

"Mother of God, She Who is Quick to Hear."
Oil painting by Ariane.
Ariane hopes her painting of this famous Western-style icon at St. Tikhons Monastery in Pennsylvania reminds people to always pray and never forget God in their lives. Postcard copies of the painting by Ariane were given to orphans in Serbia and Kosovo.

ПРЕПОД. МАТИ
SAINT

ПАРАСКЕВА
PARASKEVA

"St. Petka"
Oil painting by Ariane.
St. Petka is Ariane's Slava Saint.

Ariane with Serbian Bishop Longin promoting her humanitarian cause,
"High Fives for Kosovo," rebuilding Serbian churches and monasteries.

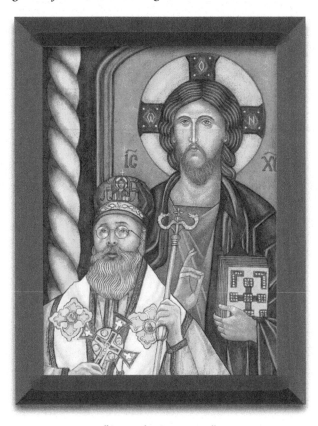

"Apostolic Succession"
Portrait of Serbian Bishop Longin. Oil painting by Ariane.

"Weep for Kosovo"
Portrait of Patriarch Pavle. Oil painting by Ariane.

Ariane hopes her artwork raises awareness for persecuted Christians in Kosovo
and around the world. Ariane's portrait of Patriarch Pavle is now on
display at his childhood home museum in Slavonia.

113

In July 2016, Ariane receives the blessing of His Grace Bishop Longin to publish her book.
Pictured left to right are: Father Serafim Baltic, Abbott of New Gracanica Monastery,
His Grace Bishop Longin, New Gracanica and Midwestern American Diocese of the Serbian
Orthodox Church, Ariane, and Father Marko Matic, parish priest at
St. Sava Serbian Orthodox Church in Merrillville, Indiana.

Ariane and her mother, 2015.
Danica is holding the brass Orthodox cross made by her late husband
and Ariane's father, Aleksandar.

Ariane treasures every moment with her mother Danica (after her stroke), 2016.

"...misery cannot exist where there is love."
St. Seraphim of Sarov

CHAPTER

VII

A Cloud of Witnesses

"Wherefore seeing we also are compassed about with so great a cloud of witnesses, let us lay aside every weight, and the sin which doth so easily beset us, and let us run with patience the race that is set before us, Looking unto Jesus the author and finisher of our faith; who for the joy that was set before him endured the cross, despising the shame, and is set down at the right hand of the throne of God."

Hebrews 12:1-2 (KJV)

I love this verse *[on the chapter title page]*. Overcoming sin is difficult; we are all flawed and we make mistakes. But if we keep our eyes on Christ, we can finish this life as spiritual champions, because the Saints are here to help us. We are *surrounded* by them like a cloud!

This verse is so Orthodox, too. Worship in heaven is continuous, but when we are in church, we are joining that heavenly worship. In church, we can see Christ and the Theotokos, the Virgin Mary, as icons on both sides of the altar. Over the altar and throughout the church, we see the Saints surrounding us in worship. They are bathed in gold, or their halos are filled with gold representing the fullness of God's grace, His uncreated light. Icons are truly windows into heaven, and they transport us into the presence of God during the Divine Liturgy.

The Saints are with us always though, and learning to open my heart and mind to their presence has transformed my life. I always start my day with readings from *Daily Lives, Miracles, and Wisdom of the Saints and Fasting Calendar* published annually by the Orthodox Calendar Company. Each page outlines the Saints commemorated on that day and then offers a quote which is always a spiritual jewel. On May 9, 2015, I read this quote and it really made an impression on me.

Elder Arsenius, the Cave-Dweller, said, "When we read the lives of the Saints, we gain two things. Firstly, the example of their struggles wakes us from numbness of negligence, and secondly, when we read the lives of the Saints with reverence, the Saints intercede to Christ for us. Before beginning to read, we must always pray. When we read the life of a Saint, it can affect us so deeply that we can't control our tears. This happens because prayer enlightens the mind."

What a beautiful concept. The Saints are like a spiritual alarm clock to wake us up, and they intercede for us with our Lord! I ask people to pray for me all the time, but knowing that the Saints who worship in heaven before the throne of God are praying for me is such a comforting thought!

I've shared with you some of the pillars of Serbian Orthodox spirituality, but there are many more Saints who have come into my life, and they are now my constant companions. I want you to know them too.

After the dove visited me, several Russian Saints became instrumental in my spiritual growth. Earlier in the book, I mentioned St. Elizabeth, who died a martyr in the Bolshevik revolution. St. John Maximovitch, who was of Serbian descent, left Russia after the communist take-over to complete his religious education in Belgrade, Yugoslavia. He became a leader in the Russian Orthodox Church Outside Russia (ROCOR) and served as Archbishop in China, France, and the United

States. St. John led the San Francisco Diocese until his death in 1966. His relics are at the cathedral in San Francisco that he helped build.

After reading his biography,[1] St. John touched the depths of my heart more than any Saint in my life after St. Elizabeth. He is called the Wonderworker because of the many miracles associated with him. After his death, he appeared to one of his devoted servants and proclaimed that even though he was dead, he was still "alive." God's grace continues to work through him!

During his life, St. John Maximovitch was acknowledged to be a holy man and living Saint. He lived in a world of prayer, contemplation, and constant communion with God. He knew all the lives of the Saints by heart; when he approached an icon or holy image in church, it seemed as if he was greeting a personal friend or relative, although heavenly. He worked to subject his will to God, as well. To develop discipline, he spent forty years of his life never sleeping in a bed.

When St. John the Wonderworker came into my life, I examined my priorities and truly wanted to put God first in my life. I wished I could talk to St. John though, because I needed more direction. I felt like a ship that was sailing along nicely on the waters of life, but I had no real destination. In his biography, there is a story about St. John appearing to one of his parishioners in a dream to deliver him a message. I prayed that he might do the same and speak to me in my dreams and tell me how I could use my gifts to glorify God.

I believe he did. Not long thereafter, I dreamed of a short monk who spoke to me from a distance. I couldn't make out his face, but in my heart, I knew it was St. John Maximovitch. He told me to look for a very specific book in an Orthodox catalogue that I kept in the kitchen. I immediately started browsing until I found it. It was *Consoler of Suffering Hearts*, a book about St. Rachel of Borodino, another Russian Saint, and I knew nothing about her.

I ordered the book and read it in two days. I was drawn to her so deeply.

St. Rachel lived in nineteenth century Russia, but she lived long enough to witness the dark days of Lenin's revolution and the rise of atheistic communism in her homeland. Most of her days in service to God were at Borodino Women's Monastery of the Savior in Moscow. The Holy Spirit moved through her in ways that I could certainly understand. The gift of vivid, even spiritual dreaming has been with me since childhood. And here was a Saint…and God spoke to her, particularly through Bogorodica (the Virgin Mary).

The book is filled with stories of visions and miracles, but there is one story that stood out to me because it shows that God is present, even in the most mundane of our labors. Mother Rachel, as she was called, frequently prepared meals in the monastery kitchen as part of her obedience, and according to visitors she was quite an extraordinary cook. But one day, when she was baking pies, the Mother of God appeared and startled her to the point of almost dropping the pies. Bogorodica kept her from stumbling and in a loving voice said, "You always ask me to help you; know that I always listen to your prayers and I bless all your labors because of your deep faith and non-hypocritical love for people."[2]

St. Rachel talked with the Saints just like we talk to everyday friends and family. It was like she had an "open line" with heaven. People today sometimes read these stories with doubt in their hearts. We don't want to believe in every-day miracles. Everything needs to be explained. But for Mother Rachel, the lines between this physical world and the unseen spiritual realm were virtually non-existent.

Protestants have wrung all the mystery out of Christianity. It's all about what you believe and having a "relationship with Jesus" and it's all very rational. But the ways of God and the holy sacraments are mystery. You can't explain how the Holy Spirit works. And when you read about the Saints with supernatural abilities, there is no explanation other than their attainment of God's grace. God is mystery.

St. Rachel was such a free spirit, she showed me that God works in many ways and it isn't always "inside the box." She showed me how REAL the Saints are and that I can speak to them always, in or out of church. She drew me into the treasury of Saints who are alive in spirit and active in this world. St. Rachel inspired me to cultivate relationships with them through a rich prayer life that is so very personal.

Consoler of Suffering Hearts changed my perspective on life. St. Rachel is also an example of God using clairvoyance and other gifts in His people. These are gifts not be sought out, and it was reassuring to me to read about others who knew how to let God use them for His glory. I just needed to stay focused on Him, and this book offered the direction I needed. St. John knew this was the perfect book to inspire me!

I can't explain how or why I have the dreams with spiritual insight. Starting with the first dream about my grandfather after he died, they always take me by surprise. The unconscious mind is still a mystery to scientists. But this gift, like having an antenna that can pick up things from other realms, must be a family trait. My mother has the gift as well. As previously discussed, some of my ancestors have explored the psychic arts. It explains my attraction to New Age practices over a portion of my adult life.

But now I understand that gifts can be used as blessings from God, or they can be exploited by darker forces, even if they seem innocent. In my post-New Age dedication to the Orthodox Church, I can only serve Christ as my master and I can only be a vessel for the Holy Spirit, like St. Rachel, as long as I bend my will to God and keep a pure heart.

The book helped me to see this clearly. In Chapter 13, "The Gifts of Clairvoyance and Miracles," the author shares over forty stories of her counsels with visitors to the monastery. As I read, it was like she was speaking to me. One woman asked her about reincarnation and after an explanation of the dry bones of Ezekiel 37, St.

Rachel spoke directly to the subject. "It is heresy," she said. "The spirit only enters into its own body."[3] Well that hit me like a hammer!

St. Rachel helped me see spiritual gifts from God's point-of-view. He speaks to people in many ways. It's not like hearing a voice out loud like Moses must have heard when God spoke to him in the burning bush on Mt. Sinai. One day, I was walking through my bedroom and passed a picture of Elder Sophrony, an Orthodox Holy Elder, on our bookcase. Suddenly, a thought just came to me out of nowhere that said, "Work at being a Christian, Ariane." That wasn't my thought. Where did that come from? I was even offended a bit. I thought I was a good person so what did this mean? Only over time was I able to understand what God was telling me through Elder Sophrony. Being a "good Christian" is not good enough. Salvation is a gift of God, but we have to work out our salvation.[4] Faith without works is dead.[5] This was a point of decision for me. Sporadic attendance at church was not enough; I needed to be in God's presence on a regular basis, even when I didn't feel like it. I needed to take communion to nourish my soul. I immersed myself into the liturgical calendar and began learning about the Saints, the cloud of witnesses. I learned to pray more by using prayer books during devotional time and saying "The Jesus Prayer" while I'm painting or working around the house.[6]

During this time of my life I had many dreams guiding me and they are too numerous to describe. As I began to align myself with the church calendar, however, the dreams began to subside. I remember the last two dreams I had about being a Christian. One was "read the Gospel of Luke, Ariane." That was it…a short and sweet message. But it was helpful because I was reading so many books about the lives of the Saints, I was neglecting to read the Bible. The last dream said, "Ariane from this time forward, put God first in ALL things." That last dream was bittersweet because I had so many interesting spiritual dreams. I knew this was the last significant message to guide me. I cannot explain why, I just felt it. Maybe God was telling me that His Word and His Holy Church were sufficient to guide me as long as I kept my focus on the right place.

Jesus said to "abide in me"[7] and the Church he established empowers you to do this. Abiding in Christ by immersing myself into the life of the Church and its Saints has certainly changed me. I'm more centered. I'm more at peace. And it has made me a better wife, mother, and daughter because I live to serve others.

Everyone who has been a care-giver to an elderly parent knows how stressful it can be. And even though I have been blessed with great people who have assisted with Mommy's care, I can promise you that I would not have made it this far without the help of our Lord and His dear Saints. As Elder Arsenius reminds us, the Saints are there to intercede for us…and I have learned to pray to them for the help I need in my most difficult times.

When my mother began her descent into vascular dementia, it put me in very uncomfortable places. I was insecure about making decisions, and suddenly I was faced with selling her home, putting on an estate sale, and finding an assisted living facility that she would find comfortable and welcoming. A friend of mine, Linda Bell, told me, "In this journey of taking care of your Mom, you will learn how to completely trust God for everything." At first, her comment hurt my feelings. I thought I already trusted God for everything in my life. My life was rooted in the church, and I strived to teach this to my kids. But she was right. I had never felt such a lack of control with events in my life, and I had no one to show me what to do. So in my desperation, I turned completely to God.

Then came the dreaded phone call in the middle of the night. "We cannot do anything to help your mom," the voice from assisted living said. "You need to come get her and move her elsewhere." It was 1 AM, and I got in my car and drove into town while praying to God for help. I wished I could take Mama home with me, but our house didn't have a ground-level room for her. Nor did I have the support I needed.

When I got there, I found my beautiful mother wearing only a table cloth and lying on a bench in the middle of the hallway with no one there to help. The staff just stared at me, waiting to see what I would do. I didn't know what I would do. All I knew was I needed to love her. I approached Mama and got down on my knees and began to sob. I could not help myself. It was an awful feeling. My beautiful mother was so helpless…Lord help us! All I could do was cry and repeat over and over, "Volim te Mama (I love you Mama)." There was nothing else to say.

Then in perfect Serbian Mama said, "Ja sam niko i ništa, Ja hoću da umrem," which means, "I am nothing and nobody. I want to die." That moment in time is etched in my memory forever; she was right, because *we are all nothing and nobody without God.* I told her again how much I loved her. I would help her and not to worry. I would always be there for her. I would not give up on her.

Then I asked her to get up and she did very easily, and we walked to her room and I dressed her for bed. We hugged and talked about our family. I told her how proud I was of her, my father, and everyone in our family. Then I put on some Serbian folk music, and she peacefully and happily fell fast asleep. Praise God!

This was just the beginning of our difficulties at the assisted living facility though. The director wanted to move Mama to the psychiatric unit as soon as possible. It was all business. There was no admission of any failings on their part. They didn't seem to really care.

This stress caused vivid dreaming that night. I saw a path in a wheat field, and I heard a woman's voice warning me about the facility director. And then I dreamed of my parents when they were together in the prime of their lives. They were handsomely dressed and reunited. Then they turned their backs to me and disappeared.

I guess I was afraid I was about to lose my mother, too, but until I had a better plan, I agreed to move her to the psych unit. It didn't go well, of course. They just pumped her full of drugs.

I wished there was another way. In January, 2014, when it was time to celebrate Nativity (Christmas) at St. Petka Serbian Orthodox Church, I wanted to take Mama to Liturgy. Everyone said it was a bad idea, including my husband. Mother was too drugged. The medications even made her hunched like a cripple. But I started praying to St. Petka, my family's patron Saint. "This is your church…please help me take my dear Mama to Liturgy once more," I prayed. That night, I dreamed of St. Petka, and she looked right at me, giving me strength.

It was bitterly cold that day and against everyone's advice, I got my mother in the van and we headed to church. We had no problems at all. My young daughter was with us, and it was such a lovely service. Mama's legs weakened on the way out of church, but there was dear Leonidas, the church's lead chanter, who picked her up and carried her back to the van to go home. St. Petka was with us!

Things have changed drastically since then. Tony and I added a room onto our house for Mama, and now she lives with us. So long, assisted living! Gone are all the psychiatric drugs and she has improved tremendously. Other than a set-back when she fell and broke her hip, we are managing with God's help and are looking forward to our next Slavas together. Just recently, she walked up nine steps into our house with minimal help! Her progress is amazing! The Saints are watching over us.

CHAPTER

VIII

WEAVING MY WAY BACK TO GOD

"*Rasti, rasti moj zeleni bore. (Grow, grow my green pine.).*"
Serbian folk song

When you hear about so many conflicts in the world, you can't help but ask, "Why can't people just get along?" (Or at least just leave each other alone!) Afghanistan, Iraq, and Syria bleed from civil war and the struggle with radical Islam. Israelis and Palestinians are in constant conflict. Serbia has had its share of conflicts with Islamic nationalism as well, and the last war in Kosovo in 1999 drew the West into the struggle. There are many misunderstandings about Kosovo even today.

Without getting into divisive ethnic politics, let's just say that Kosovo (southeast of Serbia) is a disputed territory. It was part of Serbia in the Middle Ages, as I have shared in an earlier chapter, during which time it became a significant center of Serbian Orthodox spirituality. Some call it the "Serbian Jerusalem." Kosovo includes 1,300 churches and monasteries and many of them were built during this era by Serbian kings. When you consider that Kosovo contains only 4,000 square miles, that's one monastery per every three square miles of territory!

Many of them are designated as UNESCO World Heritage Sites or as Serbian Monuments of Culture of Exceptional Importance (or both) because of their age, architecture, and priceless icons and frescoes. Most still have an active presence of Orthodox monks and nuns. Monasteries like Dečani, Gračanica, and the Patriarchate of Peć have made significant contributions to our Orthodox heritage. The Monastery of the Holy Archangels in southern Kosovo is of symbolic importance too. Serbian Tsar Dušan (1331-1355) founded the monastery and planted a pine tree there in 1336; it grew into an enormous tree towering over eighty feet and became a powerful symbol of Serbian Kosovo. The region of the Šar Mountains is known for its biological diversity including the hearty pine.

Kosovo (and later Serbia) was lost, of course, to the Ottoman Empire when St. Lazar and his troops were martyred for the Christian faith in 1389 on a polje (field or plain) surrounded by Black Pines, which began 400 years of Turkish oppression. Serbia won back its independence in the nineteenth century and in the First Balkan War of 1912, Kosovo was liberated from the Turks. Kosovo territory was then shared by the Kingdoms of Serbia and Montenegro.

Kosovo, under Serbia and later Yugoslavia, remained multi-ethnic, but in modern times, Albanian immigration made the region mostly Muslim, which set up the 1999 conflict with Serbia under President Slobodan Milošević. Fueled by the Kosovo Liberation Army (KLA), the war pitted ethnic Albanians seeking independence against minority Serbs, backed by Serbian police and paramilitary. At first, Albanians were persecuted and many fled Kosovo, until NATO, backed by the U.S. under President Bill Clinton, intervened by bombing Serbia and Milošević into submission.

After the war, Kosovo fell under United Nations administration with KFOR (Kosovo Force) acting as peacekeepers. But then, Serbs became fair game to the KLA. Two-thirds of the 300,000 Serbs in Kosovo left in a mass exodus after the revenge killings and burning and looting started. Monasteries and churches also came under attack; some seventy were destroyed or desecrated, including the historic Holy Archangels, where militants cut down and burned Tsar Dušan's ancient pine tree. They burned the stump, too, just for good measure.

In 2008, Kosovo declared its independence, but it is still not recognized by the entire international community, including Serbia, of course. Tensions continue as Serbs remaining there are concentrated in a few small regions or sectors. Harassment, even of schoolchildren, is frequent. The monasteries remain under attack even though KFOR is supposed to be protecting them.

It's a sad state of affairs for Orthodoxy in Kosovo, especially since the Serbian Orthodox Church condemned the policies of Slobodan Milošević and tried to mediate peace between ethnic Albanians and minority Serbs in the run-up to the 1999 war. Now, the church suffers again. It's why I became involved in the Decani Monastery Relief Fund to support the innocent victims of the war and share Christ's love.

Because of the accusations of Serbian war crimes (in Bosnia earlier and then Kosovo), many in the West perceived Serbia as the enemy or "bad guys" in this conflict, which is also sad considering Serbia was an ally to the West in both World Wars, opposing imperialism and fascism. Most Americans never understood why Kosovo mattered to Serbia anyway. Perhaps it is an overly simplistic analogy, but what if Texas declared its independence in the future when Hispanics became the majority population? America fought a great Civil War over the rights of states to secede. How would our government react to an ethnic campaign for independence? That is what happened in Kosovo.

What's done is done, but for me, it's important to keep my faith first and not get distracted by other issues. For many Serbs, the passions fueled by nationalism can run high. But we must be careful, because hatred and racism can sometimes get intertwined with patriotism and national pride. A flower can become choked with weeds if the garden is not well tended.

St. Sava, Serbia's founder of church and state, was a passionate defender of Orthodoxy, but he hated no one. He lived in a time where there was a great struggle for territory between kingdoms and spheres of influence between Rome and Constantinople. Latin Crusaders even occupied his beloved Mt. Athos in Greece, and he still showed them nothing but love and hospitality. St. Sava didn't judge anyone; he just loved Orthodoxy above all. And in the end, everyone, including Roman Catholics, Jews, and Muslims, respected him as a holy man.

Another great Serbian Saint is St. Basil of Ostrog, who lived during the seventeenth century during the time of Ottoman rule. He was a man of extreme humility who served the Church as both a monk and bishop. After his death, his relics were kept for the veneration of the faithful at Ostrog Monastery, which he founded. The upper monastery was carved out of the side of steep cliffs, but Orthodox and Catholic Christians, and even Muslims, make the difficult pilgrimage to pray at his side because of the miracles that occur through St. Basil's intercessions. Holiness is a light that all can see.

Serbia is a small nation, but through Saints such as Sava and Lazar, God has called it to be a Christian people. God's children must suffer and endure to be purified, however. Under the Old Covenant, the Hebrew nation was enslaved in Egypt for 400 years. Israel has suffered through conquests, exiles, and even attempts at extermination in modern times. The Orthodox of little Serbia have shared a similar fate under the New Covenant.

St. Justin Popović challenges all Serbs to examine their faith. In a homily on Vidovdan, he cried that too many Serbs have forgotten Holy Serbia. He said, "If you are a true Serb, if the St. Sava of Serbia heart beats in you, you are fully with Christ the Lord. Fully with His truth in this world and the next. You are fully with Holy Prince Lazar, you fully die in Kosovo for the Honorable Cross and freedom which is golden."[1]

His teacher, St. Nikolai Velimirović, echoed, "No one can be a good Serb without first being a good man. But there is no force in the world, nor has there ever been, which could make one good, other than the force of Christ's faith. So, don't wish for Serbdom without substance."[2]

These words should shake every Christian out of apathy. Too many of us think of our faith as just another form of identity. We are Americans. Christians. Republicans or Democrats. Conservatives or Liberals. They are all labels we put on ourselves. Catholic. Greek Orthodox. On and On. No matter who you are or where you were born or how you were raised, can you put your faith in Christ above all? That is what Saints Justin and Nikolai were telling their fellow Serbs to do. Our devotion to Christ must be above nationalism, patriotism, materialism, and all other "isms."

As a Serbian American, before I completely reawakened to my Orthodox faith, I didn't really understand the significance of Kosovo. But like so many other personal revelations, God revealed it to me in a dream. This one was intense. It was twilight and I was driving in a convertible MG with a friend from church on a wet road when suddenly the car went airborne for twenty or thirty feet! I looked back and saw a white box in the road that I flew over and missed somehow. I started singing "Holy God, Holy Almighty, Holy Immortal" thinking it was the end of us, but the car miraculously landed gently back on the road. I looked back again and there was a woman clinging to the trunk of the car extending to me her hand. While still squeezing the steering wheel, I desperately reached back to grab her, and I noticed her fist tightly clutching a pine branch that was whipping in the wind. I didn't know how long I could hold onto her, but I was hanging on for dear life!

This was confusing, and I couldn't forget the dream. I called my best girlfriend Jennie Atty Gelles in Kentucky. What can a pine branch possibly mean? I started reading. Then I discovered the story of the pine tree planted by Tsar Dušan at Holy Archangels Monastery in Kosovo and its mighty span lasting almost 700 years. And then I read again about King Aleksandar I. As Crown Prince, he fought for the liberation of Kosovo in the First Balkan War. He inherited the throne in 1921 and five years later, he returned to Holy Archangels Monastery to place a memorial plaque at Tsar Dušan's magnificent pine tree.

Aleksandar served as Yugoslavia's king for thirteen years until his life and reign were cut short by an assassin in France. When they brought his body back to Yugoslavia, he was buried at Oplenac, in the mausoleum of the Karadjordjević dynasty. As part of his military funeral procession, peasants brought a pine branch from Kosovo Polje. When I read that, it took my breath away! The pine is a powerful symbol of my Serbian heritage. I think God was telling me to cling to my Serbian roots, my family, and my Orthodox faith…and to know what they mean. *The pine branch in the dream was the thread that brings me and my people back to the gift of St. Lazar!* Now I understand!

This all came together for me as I painted a portrait of St. Nikolai Velimirović. I'm a portrait painter, not an iconographer, so I can use more creative license in my works. As I started painting, I included the church he built in his home village of Lelić in the background, but as I continued I added a pine branch and a ribbon of the Serbian flag to connect him with Kosovo's spiritual heritage. A framed, hand-signed, giclée-on-canvas print of the painting is now at Dević Monastery, a convent for women near Srbica, Kosovo, that was burned and desecrated by an Albanian mob. Abbess Anastasia cried when Father Nektarios Serfes, representing the Decani Monastery Relief Fund, presented her with the painting in 2014.

That very same year, I was honored with a Gramota Ecclesiastical Award for my work from Bishop Teodosije of Raška-Prizren and Kosovo-Metohija. I was deeply moved by this recognition.

I am not a famous painter, nor — in all likelihood — will I ever be; but I am deeply humbled that one of my paintings is at a monastery in Kosovo. A more recent painting I made of the Mother of God called "She Who Is Quick to Hear" was printed as cards and given to orphans in Belgrade and Serbian children in Kosovo by the Lifeline Humanitarian Organization with care package items to remind them that our Lord's mother is always interceding for us in prayer. Lifeline was founded by Her Royal Highness Crown Princess Katherine Karadjordjević of Serbia and I was so thrilled that my friend Melanie Gruyich Sever, who works with the organization, included the prints in the outreach to children.

The original icon, "She Who Is Quick to Hear," was given by monks on Mt. Athos to St. Tikhon Monastery in Pennsylvania, where St. Nikolai served as dean and rector of its seminary in his last days. Father Nektarios remembers this miraculous icon at St. Tikhon's very well. So it has a rich history that many of us cherish.

Another blessing — I was recently informed that one of my paintings has been chosen to hang in a permanent exhibition in the childhood house museum of Serbian Patriarch Pavle, who reposed in 2009. Wow. Glory to God!

God has blessed me with ways to contribute my talents to the work of His Holy Church. As I browse through pictures in my family album, I feel like I have truly taken my place in our Orthodox tradition which is being passed down from "generation to generation." The threads in my life have woven me completely into our tapestry of faith.

My dear mother is so proud of our heritage…almost to a fault at times, because her family served a king who served Christ. This is a foreign notion to Americans, but the idea of God appointing kings goes back to the Old Testament when the Prophet Samuel anointed Saul as the first King of Israel. That concept of divine appointment carried over into Christendom. The Church anointed the Emperors of Byzantium. St. Sava anointed his brother Stefan as the first King of Serbia. This tradition was still in place when King Aleksandar took the throne of Yugoslavia in 1921; he was crowned in church.

Members of my mother's family served King Aleksandar. Her Aunt/Teta Radmila's husband, Miloš Dragović, was a senator in the king's government. His brother also was head of the forestry department under the king. They were servants of the king who was a servant of God, so there is a regal lineage in the family. It says a lot in terms of my family's position prior to World War II. I think that's why Mama took me to Oplenac on our last trip together to Yugoslavia in 1987. She wanted me to see King Aleksandar's tomb and know our personal history with Yugoslav royalty.

Our family lost everything in that terrible war. Mama's uncle, the senator, paid for his loyalty to the crown when the communists picked him up in 1943, and he died in prison. Her father, Velibor (which means big pine), left the country for the U.S. after the war, so her mother Darinka constantly worked to support the children left behind. The extended family became more important, and I think that is how Teta Rada became like a surrogate mother to Mama. As the daughter of an Orthodox priest (whose murder by Bulgarians was covered in Chapter 7), Aunt Rada prayed for Mama constantly as well. Teta Rada has always stood out as one of the most influential members of our family because of her devotion as an Orthodox Christian.

It is through her that I believe Mama learned to pray so diligently for her family in church. We Orthodox pray for the living and the dead, the latter to keep their memory alive. She, in turn, has taught me the responsibility of keeping these prayers going. She remembers four generations of her family during Slava celebration every year, and now I have inherited her very long list. My mother has shared their stories with me, and it truly feels like all of our ancestors are with us when we light the candles and speak their names in prayer. They are with us in the Divine Liturgy, just as the Saints and angels are, worshipping God.

Teta Rada must still be fervently praying for Mama in heaven too, because she remains a guide to us in mother's dreams. I've already shared the story of when she appeared to Mama to warn her of my father's death. Aunt Rada came to her in another dream that disturbed her deeply.

This occurred when my mother was living in her home alone. She was in a dispute with her neighbor about her dog Marko's barking. Yes, the dog was named after Kraljević Marko, the medieval Serbian Prince (smile). She was offended, and I guess she wanted to prove that she was a successful, hard-working American citizen because she called me and asked me to frame a picture of the five houses she owned since moving to this country. I thought to myself, "Oh boy, here we go with more drama!" I knew she was just hurt and lonely though, so I let her continue with the tirade.

The next day she called back in a very tender and hurt voice asking me to come over so she could tell me about a frightful dream she had. I dropped the kids off for school, picked up two green teas, and drove over to her house not sure of what was going to happen next.

Mama said the dream started with a voice saying, "Get up Danica Dobric Trifunovic!" And then she pointed to a corner of the room and said Teta Rada was there. Aunt Rada motioned for her to look into another corner of the room where there was an imposing presence that frightened her. This being spoke. "Why do you know of me, but don't know me?" he asked. This gave me chills as I looked around at the icons and crosses in her bedroom. Then he asked Mama, "Why do you leave your home with a bitter countenance? Be of good cheer when you exit! You may have had five homes, but soon you will have none!"

Mommy woke up suddenly and the dream was so real, she thought someone had broken into the house and was still there in the room with her. She sat up in bed and asked aloud, "What time is it?" She heard the voice again answer, "2 AM." She looked at the clock beside her bed. It was exactly 2 AM.

The dream scared her, but in a good way. My mother's pride can become imbalanced, and she can be angry when she feels insulted. I believe it was our Lord Jesus Christ speaking to her in the dream, reprimanding her out of love. And I believe he was summoned by my most pure, virtuous Great Aunt Rada. I feel that Teta Rada continues to pray for my mother's soul and for her salvation. Her picture remains by my mother's bed.

The dream may have been disturbing to Mommy, but it was comforting to me. We are not alone in our struggles. It was also prophetic. Within a year, I sold her last two homes and most of her possessions.

Caring for my aging mother, as I have matured through my own spiritual reawakening, has given me a much needed perspective of her. As much as she has taught me good things about our faith and family, I see her faults as well. She has always been broad-minded, confident, and beautiful with a timeless elegance. But she could also be bitter and unforgiving. She was proud of her heritage, but her pride was often a stumbling block. Because my father died when I was 18, she has been the dominant family member in my life. She has been there with me in all the important steps in my life, but at times she has shut me out as well. I have learned to forgive and understand…and be grateful for the best things she has given me.

Even when it's hopeless, there is always hope with my mother. It's in her name, as Mama frequently explained. Zvezda Danica means "morning star." What a beautiful name. In Revelation 22:16 (KJV), Jesus says, "I am the root and the offspring of David, and the bright and morning star." The planet Venus is the morning star, of course, and it has been important to every culture observing the heavens throughout antiquity. When you see the morning star, you know sunrise is soon to follow. It may be dark, but the light of day is almost here! Christ is always our hope, our redemption.

I was thinking about this the other day while driving and a TobyMac song came on the radio. "Undeniable" is about God's presence in our lives. When I heard the chorus, I couldn't help but smile and turn up the volume.

> "Undeniable, You are, You are, You are
> Unmistakable, You are, You are
> You're the bright and morning star
> But still You speak to my heart"[3]

Our Lord is undeniable and unmistakable. I see him working in my life every day. His presence and the company of his Saints warm my heart.

The rediscovery of my Orthodox heritage has led me to deeper waters in the Christian faith, and it has changed me in many ways. I'm keenly aware of my Master and I want to obey His will as his handmaiden. Following Christ is all-consuming for me as I take up my cross daily. My parents and ancestors armed me with a faith that has stood the test of time…the Orthodox Christian Faith, the Pravoslavna Vera. And I pray my children and the generations that follow will do the same until Christ returns for his bride, the Church.

I hope my story leads you to a deeper, more meaningful walk with Christ as well. So many Christians live their lives in the "wading pool" of shallow faith and minimal knowledge. Step into the deep end and walk towards Jesus and let your faith hold you up! If you sink, like St. Peter, the Lord will take you by the hand![4]

Some of you may want to learn more about the Orthodox Christian Church. Others, who were born into the church like me, may want to follow my path and become more devout in the faith we inherited. Orthodoxy is open to *all people*. Speak to a local priest and let him guide you. It is the ancient Christian faith, but it's more relevant than ever.

Perhaps reading this book is part of your *sudbina* or destiny. Serbs understand the meaning of the Serbian word sudbina as the will of God. It's not the same thing as fate. Sudbina is the path in life that God has intended for you. Serbian Orthodox do not question the will of God. The Father always knows what's best for us, and He has the final say.

God's perfect will for *all of us* is to leave our sins behind and turn to Him. Look at the threads in your life… bound together, they could be leading you to a deeper commitment to Christ and a life of devotion within the Orthodox Church. Living a life in daily communion with Jesus Christ and all of his glorious Saints was *my* sudbina. Perhaps, it is *yours* too!

In an ever-changing world, the Orthodox Church is a witness to the one unchanging truth that God became one of us in the person of Jesus Christ, so that we might become like Him through His saving grace. And even if the whole world stands against us, we must hold firm to this truth for the "Honorable Cross and Freedom which is Golden." It is *our sudbina* — our destiny according to God — to struggle to preserve our holy Orthodox Christian faith, from *generation to generation*, until the end. Amen! Amin!

The End, and Glory to Thee!
Kraj, i Bogu našem Slava!

REFLECTIONS
EPILOGUE

TIM WEEKS

TIM WEEKS
EPILOGUE

As a word of introduction, I have worked in Nashville for over twenty-five years as a writer and independent television/film producer. I did not expect to co-author a book about Serbian Orthodox spirituality.

I have been Orthodox for sixteen years now. Raised Southern Baptist, I didn't expect to become Orthodox. Life can have some interesting turns if you are open to how the Spirit moves. A Southern native, I was not exposed to Orthodoxy at all growing up; I never came into contact with it. But in my late thirties, I began asking questions, which began a fascinating journey. First of all, let me say I am grateful for how I was raised. My parents were church-going, moral people, and the Bible was taught and discussed in our home. We attended church twice on Sundays. Baptists had Training Union and Sunday night services too. And if that wasn't enough, we frequently watched Bible teachers like Jerry Falwell and Charles Stanley on TV on Sunday nights. Whew.

When I made it into my thirties though, I tired of "getting saved" sermons and started thinking there had to be more to Christianity. I began attending a Presbyterian Church in my neighborhood and decided that was where I needed to be. The services were more formal, the sermons were more thought-provoking, and the church was very involved in community service and outreach programs.

It was during this time that the Presbyterian USA denomination (like other mainline Protestants) began debating gay marriage and gay clergy. It was divisive of course, but I wondered aloud why issues of such important theological consequences were up for a vote. That is the nature of Protestant churches. Always changing. Always splintering. If you don't like what's going on, just start something else. There are hundreds of denominations now. And if you don't like them, you can be "non-denominational." That seems to be the most popular trend these days. People turned off by theology are attracted to churches that offer entertaining music and more casual fellowship.

It was also at this time that I became interested in learning church history. In the Baptist church, it's like it didn't exist…or matter at all. There were Jesus and the apostles to read about…and then you fast forward to you, me, and Billy Graham. When you join the Presbyterian Church, they at least give you a primer on the Reformation and the beginning of the Protestant movement led by Luther and Calvin. So by the sixteenth century, you knew there were problems with the Catholic Church. But what about before that? Just when did Christianity get "off track" and in need of reform? Those types of questions intrigued me. I knew very little of the first fifteen centuries of church history.

So this was my new hobby, reading about how we got from Jesus Christ to the Reformation, and I found a lot of interesting material. One thing I learned was Christianity thrived in Ireland, Scotland, and England for a number of centuries in the first millennium without any ecclesiastical supervision from the Pope in Rome. The Roman Empire retreated at the beginning of the fifth century, and Christianity was on its own. But it became the dominant religion through missionary Saints like St. Patrick, St. Columba, and St. Cuthbert. After the time of St. Patrick, monasteries (influenced greatly by the Desert Fathers of Egypt) were founded, many in remote places, and from there, the monks evangelized the countryside by preaching, ministering, and building churches. The monastic tradition of early Christianity in the West got my attention. Luther and Calvin abolished monasticism for Protestants. So was Christianity already getting "off track" at this early stage in church history?

I began corresponding with a person who was involved in a revival of "Celtic Christianity." In an email he told me that the theology behind the ancient Celtic prayers I was reading was more Orthodox than Catholic. The emphasis was on "theosis" or deification. It was salvation by transformation, not the legalistic justification which dominates western theology. This was my first contact with Orthodoxy…after three years of studying on my own. It surprised me that early Christianity in the West was actually Eastern.

Reading in a vacuum was becoming dull, so in 1997, I began attending Holy Trinity Greek Orthodox Church in Nashville occasionally, just out of curiosity. When I asked about sitting in on a catechumen class, I remember telling Father George Vaporis, "I have no intention of becoming Orthodox, but I would like to hear you talk about it, if that's ok." This began another three-year journey because contemplating the truth of Orthodoxy caused me to question everything I had been taught to believe up to that point.

While I was splitting time between the Presbyterian Church and Holy Trinity, I discovered one historical truth which was a tipping point for me. Once a month, when there was a baptism at the Presbyterian Church, I kept noticing a footnote in the bulletin that said, "Earliest records of Christian baptism describe the candidate standing in a pool of water and reciting what he believes, then being immersed." With so many variations on baptisms today, including sprinkling, I wondered, "Why did this change, and who changed it?" When I was baptized as a young boy, I didn't recite anything. I didn't say anything. The minister just dunked me a few weeks after I walked the aisle in response to an altar call and filled out a card as my "profession of faith."

The eye-opening book was "Lectures to Candidates for Baptism" by St. Cyril, who was Bishop of the Church in Jerusalem in the fourth century. I thought, "This has to be good." In his catechetical lectures, he describes everything in detail. The catechumen faces the west and renounces his sins and evil. Then he faces the east and states what he believes by reciting the Creed (the Nicene Creed, part one, was in use by then), and then he is immersed three times in the name of the Father, Son and Holy Spirit. OK, there it was — a step-by-step description of ancient Christian baptism. To my surprise, this is exactly how the Orthodox Church still baptizes people today. The sacrament is unchanged over 2,000 years of Christian history. That impressed me.

I was also impressed with the Orthodox Church's historical position on the Eucharist, or communion. Presbyterians offer communion once a month. Baptists are even more casual, offering it once a quarter. At an Orthodox Church, communion is every Sunday and is often offered during the week on other feast days. It is the reason you come to church…to partake of the body and blood of Christ. In Timothy (Kallistos) Ware's book, "The Orthodox Church," I read about St. Ignatius, who followed St. John the Apostle, as the Bishop of the Church in Antioch around 100 AD. In letters, he defined the church as "the people of God around their bishop celebrating the Eucharist." He also described communion as the "medicine of immortality." So, obviously, to early Christians, communion was not a "symbolic" remembering of the Lord's Supper. It was the real deal. Baptism was the initiation into the faith. Consuming Christ's body and blood was being joined literally to God's saving grace. It's what made you Christian.

By the year 2000, I knew there were many things I still didn't understand, but I also knew that I wanted to be Orthodox. I was attending multiple weeknight services during Lent. I was there every night during Holy Week and Pascha. People were fasting. There were many hours of prayer. I thought, "These people are serious about their faith." I felt connected to all of the ancient traditions and rituals.

By late summer, I paid a visit to Father George in his office. I told him that I would become Orthodox if I could ever articulate why I should be Orthodox. I let him read a letter I had written to my pastor at the Presbyterian Church. Father said, "I think you're ready." The letter was never mailed, but Father George baptized me on October 8, 2000, according to the ritual I had read about.

People come to Orthodoxy in different ways. Many are born into the church, like Ariane. Being baptized as Orthodox doesn't save you, though. Like people in all churches, some don't remain in the faith. Others slip into a pattern of casual attendance without ever learning the deeper meaning of living a Christ-like life. Thankfully, many Orthodox are committed Christians who actively practice their faith. Some of them come back into the life of the church after drifting away for a time.

The Orthodox Church includes "converts." Some are married into the church. Many others are drawn to it from other traditions, like me. The movement by people from so many diverse backgrounds into Orthodoxy can only be the work of the Holy Spirit. It is people "coming home" to the truth. At my church, I see young people who are enthusiastic about becoming Orthodox. With American culture shifting to entertaining mega-churches or no church at all, it's refreshing to see a new generation seeking out a faith that is real.

Others come to Orthodoxy with no church background at all. Such is the story of Father Serafim Baltic, the Serbian Orthodox monk and abbot mentioned in this book. Born in 1978, he grew up as an ethnic-Serb living in Croatia during the waning days of communism and the break-up of Yugoslavia. In communist-controlled schools, atheism was prevalent. Father Serafim only discovered the Orthodox Church, the church of his Serbian heritage, after he immigrated to the U.S. and attended college in Florida. Time spent at a Greek Orthodox monastery in central Florida inspired him to commit his life to church service.

Everyone has a unique story of their faith journey, but we share only one truth as a common destination. The Orthodox Church is the original church founded by Jesus Christ that has not wavered in its theology or traditions over 2,000 years of Christian history. It is the fullness of faith.

So it's not a matter of Christianity getting off track, leading to the Reformation. If your heart is open to the truth, you will see that the Orthodox Church remained true and straight, while the church in the West steered off course and then splintered into hundreds of pieces. If it was true in the first few centuries after the time of Christ, it must be true today and always.

As we were writing this book, Ariane and I took a trip to Atlanta with Albina Murgalo, another friend of hers from St. Ignatius in Franklin. While there, we met an educated and artistic Serbian woman who invited us into her home. She had a beautiful icon of the Theotokos in her living room, but after a short conversation, it was obvious she knew very little about her own religious heritage. Over coffee, she became intrigued by how I became involved in Ariane's book project. After all, I was not Serbian. I told her that I converted to Orthodoxy. She asked plainly, "Now why would you want to do that?"

Why would I want to do that? Wow. Because the Orthodox Church shows me how to be a real Christian. How to be "in this world, but not of it."

Too much of Christianity today is either liberal, without conviction, or just another form of entertainment with rock star pastors who want you to be "fulfilled, happy, and successful." To the contrary, the historical Church is built on the witness of Saints who suffered for the truth, while emptying themselves of all worldly desires to follow Christ. The Saints of Serbia mentioned in this book are just a few examples. Our purpose in life is not for people to see us, but to see Christ instead.

This is not easy but Jesus said, "Because strait is the gate, and narrow is the way, which leadeth unto life, and few there be that find it" (Matthew 7:14 KJV). Compared to the super-highway of "easy Christianity," Orthodoxy is a narrow and very difficult path. If you are ready to humble yourself before God and open your heart to a faith which is sacramental and ascetic, then the truth preserved by the Orthodox Church will change your life.

May God bless you on your journey and I hope Ariane's story moves you closer to the Kingdom of Heaven.

Timothy (Timotheos) Weeks

ABOUT THE AUTHORS

BIOGRAPHIES

ARIANE TRIFUNOVIC MONTEMURO
TIM WEEKS

ARIANE TRIFUNOVIC MONTEMURO

Ariane Trifunovic Montemuro is a Serbian American artist who is passionate about spreading the basic law of God: *love and love alone*. She was married in St. Nicholas Serbian Orthodox Church in Philadelphia, Pennsylvania, whose grounds were blessed by one of her favorite Saints, St. Nikolai Velimirović. She is married to Anthony Montemuro, MD, and has two children, Anthony Alexander and Ana Ariane, and one beloved West Highland White Terrier, MacDuff.

Ariane holds a BA in Art History and a Masters in Teaching Museum Education; she also attended the New York School of Visual Arts, where she studied Studio Art for several years. She has had the honor of taking several iconography painting classes with the world-renown teachers of the non-profit organization Hexaemeron, and believes her paintings are strongly influenced by her love of Orthodox Christian iconography. She is also proud to be a board member of the Decani Monastery Relief Fund, a humanitarian non-profit organization that rebuilds desecrated Serbian churches and monasteries and helps the forgotten people of Kosovo.

The greatest desire of Ariane's life, other than being a wife and mother, is to serve God. Her hope is that her paintings somehow tell a story that lead people to learn more about God. Ariane has always felt that God knew how to reach her through her love of reading and books. Therefore, it is her great hope and heartfelt desire that this book, penned with Tim Weeks, is a golden thread in the reader's life, pulling him or her closer and binding them to their Creator. Hopefully, after that, she prays the reader will feel drawn to read more about the Holy Saints of God and then, most importantly, the Bible. This book is her offering to the God she loves with all her heart and her gift to her children and generations to follow....

TIM WEEKS

Tim Weeks is a film/television writer and producer based in Nashville, Tennessee. A graduate of the University of Mississippi, Tim has produced numerous documentaries, music series, and specials over his 25-year career. His documentary, "The Space Shuttle: Flying for Me" was nominated for a regional Emmy in 2015.

Tim converted to Orthodoxy in October, 2000, and feels blessed that Ariane asked him to help write her story. A regular contributor of video work to the Orthodox Christian Network from 2011-2014, Tim believes that Orthodoxy offers the fullness of faith to any Christian seeking a deeper, more meaningful spiritual walk. He and his wife Teresa are active members at Holy Trinity Greek Orthodox Church in Nashville.

REFERENCE

FOOTNOTES

RESOURCE NOTES

RESOURCES
FOOTNOTES

FORWARD

1. Ana Smiljanic, *Our Thoughts Determine Our Lives* (St. Herman Press: Platina, CA 2009), 64.

TO MY CHILDREN

1. *Akathist to the Mother of God "Nurturer of Children"* (St. Paisius Orthodox Monastery: Safford, AZ 2002), 8.

CHAPTER 1

1. Very Rev. Fr. Jovan Todorovich, *Serbian Patron Saint* (Merrillville, IN 1978), 4,7.

2. Candles symbolize prayer in Orthodox worship. When we enter the narthex of the church, we collect our thoughts and offer prayers with the lighting of candles placed before icons of Christ and the Theotokos, or Virgin Mary. Then we proceed to join the worship service, the Divine Liturgy on Sundays. With so many candles, churches provide large containers filled with sand to serve as a mass candle holder. In some churches, it is still a tradition to say prayers for the living on one side of the narthex and prayers for the deceased on the other side.

3. Victor Afanasiev, *Elder Barsanuphius of Optina* (Saint Herman Press: Platina, CA, 2000), 53.

4. Afanasiev, *Elder Barsanuphius of Optina*, 53.

CHAPTER 2

1. A censer is a clay or metal vessel for the ceremonial burning of incense. The smoke from the censer represents our prayers rising to heaven, as they did in ancient Israel as sung in Psalm 140:2 (Orthodox Study Bible)/Psalm 141: 2 (KJV).

2. "Christian writers from the time of Tertullian have testified to the practice of Christians making the 'Sign of the Lord,' that is, crossing themselves. They are doing that partly for the purpose of sanctifying every action in daily life..." Rev. Nicon D. Patrinacos, *A Dictionary of Greek Orthodoxy* (Light & Life Publishing: Minneapolis, MN, 1984), 338.

CHAPTER 3

1. Elder Cleopa of Romania, *The Truth of Our Faith: A Discourse from Holy Scripture on the Teachings of True Christianity* (Uncut Mountain Press: Tagarades, GR, 2000), Chapter 19.

2. "It is the custom in the Eastern Church to do the cross stroke from the right shoulder to the left, while in the Western Church the cross stroke is drawn from left to right." Patrinacos, *A Dictionary of Greek Orthodoxy*, 338.

3. www.orthodoxchurchquotes.com/category/sayings-from-saints-elders-and-fathers/st-nikolai-velimirovich/page/4/.

CHAPTER 4

1. My favorite book about St. Elizabeth is **Grand Duchess Elizabeth of Russia: New Martyr of the Communist Yoke** by Lubov Miller (Nikodemos Orthodox Publishing Society: Richfield Spring, NY, revised edition 2009).

2. The Cherubic Hymn is sung by the people just prior to the Great Entrance in the Orthodox Liturgy. "Just as the Cherubimic angels serve at God's throne (Ezekiel 10) and are in some mystical way part of God's movement in His temple, so now as we approach the altar to offer bread and wine to God, we serve in a similar role." Theodore Bobosh, *The Divine Liturgy according to St. John Chrysostom with Commentary and Biblical References* (Light & Life Publishing: Minneapolis, MN, 1989), 31.

3. www.thedecanifund.org.

4. "The term (relic) refers to the material remains of a Saint after his death and, in some cases, to the sacred objects which had been in contact with his body. Veneration of relics...traces of it may be found in the Old Testament. In the New Testament, there is mentioned the healing power of clothing that had been in touch with St. Paul's body (Acts 19:20). In post-New Testament times, the martyrs' bodies

were venerated from an early date. The first evidence occurs in the 'Martyrdom of St. Polycarp' (about 156–57). The relics are described as 'more valuable than precious stones and finer than refined gold' and were to be collected and honored by memorial services for the Saint." Patrinacos, *A Dictionary of Greek Orthodoxy*, 316-317.

5. www.hexaemeron.org.

6. *Hidden and Triumphant: The Underground Struggle to Save Russian Iconography* by Irina Yazykova was published in 2010 by Paraclete Press and is widely available from U.S. book sellers.

CHAPTER 5

1. A great primer about church history and Orthodox theology is *The Orthodox Church* by (Metropolitan) Timothy (Kallistos) Ware (Penguin Books: London, UK, revised edition 1997).

2. 2 Corinthians 9:24–26.

3. Father Peter Gillquist, who was a leader in the non-denominational Campus Crusade for Christ, documented the journey of Protestant Christians to the Antiochian Orthodox Church in *Becoming Orthodox* (Conciliar Press: Ben Lomond, CA, revised edition 1992). He also edited a collection of stories by leading Protestants who are now Orthodox, *Coming Home* (also Conciliar Press: Ben Lomond, CA, 1992).

4. For further reading, a good biography is *The New Chrysostom: Bishop Nikolaj Velimirović* by Vladislav Maevskii and Bishop Artemije (Radosavlijević), (St. Thikhon's Seminary Press: Waymart, PA 2011).

5. Nikolai Velimirović, *Orthodox America*, Vol. XIX (No. 5 [169]). His address is published on the web at orthodoxinfo.com/general/stnikolai_america.aspx.

6. Velimirović, *Orthodox America*.

7. Matthew 5: 13–16.

8. Matthew 24:37 and Luke 17:26.

9. Velimirović, *Orthodox America*.

10. Velimirović, *Orthodox America*.

11. Matthew 13:45–46.

CHAPTER 6

1. For a sampling of quotes from Church Fathers regarding theosis, see the Wikipedia web page, en.wikipedia.org/wiki/Divinization_(Christian).

2. Bishop Kallistos Ware, "The Spiritual Father in Saint John Climacus and Saint Symeon the New Theologian," in Irénée Hausherr's *Spiritual Direction in the Early Christian East* (Cistercian Publications/Liturgical Press: Collegeville, MN 1990), 7.

3. It may be hard to find, but a book about St. Sava given to me and my brother by our parents in 1976 remains in my library as a good resource: *Biography of Saint Sava by Mateja Matejić* (Kosovo Publishing: Columbus, OH, 11976).

4. Mateja Matejić, *Biography of Saint Sava* (Kosovo Publishing: Columbus, OH 1976), 7.

5. The story of the rich young ruler appears in three Gospels. Matthew 19:16–30, Mark 10:17–31 and Luke 18:18–30.

6. A collection of writings about Kosovo by two of Serbia's greatest modern-age Saints is *The Mystery and Meaning of the Battle of Kosovo*, by Bishop Nikolai Velimirović and Archimandrite Justin Popović (The Serbian Orthodox Metropolitante of New Gracanica: Grayslake, IL, 1999).

7. Bishop Maxim Vasilijević, "The Heavenly Kingdom in Serbia's Historic Destiny" in *The Christian Heritage of Kosovo and Metohija: The Historical and Spiritual Heartland of the Serbian People* (Sebastian Press: Los Angeles, CA 2015), 271.

8. Matthew 10:16–22, Matthew 24:9–13, Mark 13:9–13, John 15:18–16:3.

9. Matthew 16:24, Mark 8:34, and Luke 9:23.

10. Luke 23:34 KJV.

11. Bishop Nikolai Velimirović and Archimandrite Justin Popović, *The Mystery and Meaning of the Battle of Kosovo* (The Serbian Orthodox Metropolitante of New Gracanica: Grayslake, IL 1999), 120–121.

12. Father Daniel Rogich, *Serbian Patericon: Saints of the Serbian Orthodox Church* (Saint Herman Press: Platina, CA, 1994) 15.

CHAPTER 7

1.   Father Seraphim Rose, *Blessed John the Wonderworker: A Preliminary Account of the Life and Miracles of Archbishop John Maximovitch* (Saint Herman Press: Platina, CA, 1987) is a rare book now, but worth the effort if you can find it.

2.   Archpriest Sergei Lebedev, *Consoler of Suffering Hearts* (Saint Xenia Skete: Wildwood, CA, 2001), 49.

3.   Lebedev, *Consoler of Suffering Hearts*, 148.

4.   Philippians 2:12.

5.   James 2:17–18.

6.   The Jesus Prayer, "Lord Jesus Christ, Son of God, have mercy on me, a sinner," is a well-known prayer of the heart repeated frequently by Orthodox Christians. For more information, see Ware, *The Orthodox Church*, 304–306.

7.   John 15: 4–5.

CHAPTER 8

1.   Abba Justin Popović, "To The Heavenly Kingdom!," *The Path of Orthodoxy*, Vol. 50, No. 2 (Spring, 2015): 12.

2.   *Missionary Letters of Saint Nikolai Velimirovich, Letters 1–100* (New Gracanica Monastery: Grayslake, IL, 2008), 29.

3.   "Undeniable" is a bonus track on Christian hip-hop artist TobyMac's 2015 album, *This Is Not a Test*.

CPSIA information can be obtained
at www.ICGtesting.com
Printed in the USA
LVOW06s1737241016
509636LV00007B/7/P

9 781628 801316